103

Also by Donald E. Hill

God's Plan for the Local Church
Pathway of Discipleship 101
Pathway of Discipleship 102
Pathway of Discipleship 103
Pathway of Discipleship 104

PATHWAY OF DISCIPLESHIP

103

BY

DR. DONALD E. HILL

SECOND EDITION

Lay Leadership International's
DISCIPLESHIP CURRICULUM

CHRISTOS PUBLISHING COMPANY, INC.
INTERNATIONAL OFFICES: 31630 RAILROAD CANYON ROAD, SUITE 5, CANYON LAKE, CALIFORNIA 92380 U.S.A.

A *Group Leader Guide* is available for
Pathway of Discipleship 101 from
Lay Leadership International.

First edition published 1978

Second edition published 1983

All biblical quotations and printed texts unless otherwise stated, are
taken from *The Holy Bible, New International Version* © 1978 by New
York International Bible Society. Used by permission.

ISBN 0-88151-026-2 *(Pathway 101)*

ISBN 0-88151-029-7 (Set)

Printed in the United States of America

CONTENTS

Instructions vii

The Pathway of Discipleship Master Diagram viii

A Note from the Author ix

Abbreviations x

MERCY: THE ESSENTIAL RESPONSE OF DISCIPLESHIP

Lesson One   Blessed Are the Merciful 1
    I.   Introduction
    II.   What is God's Mercy?
    III. Jesus Communicated His Father's Heart
    IV. Who Are the Merciful?
    V.   A Practical Illustration of Mercy
    VI. Summation

Lesson Two   Jesus Christ: God's Mercy in Action 25
    I.   Introduction
    II.   Who Was Jesus Christ?
    III. Why Did Jesus Christ Come?
    IV. How Did Christ Accomplish His Purpose?
    V.   Summation

Lesson Three   The World-Wide Strategy of Jesus Christ 45
    I.   He Began With Himself
    II.   He Chose Twelve Men
    III. He Comissioned His Church
    IV. He Empowered His Church
    V.   Summation

Lesson Four   The Church: Christ's Body on Earth 63
    I.   What is the Church?
    II.   What is the Body of Christ?
    III. Understanding Christ's Body
    IV. The Local Expression of Christ's Body
    V.   Summation

Lesson Five   Understanding Spiritual Gifts 81
    I.   Spiritual Gifts and Grace
    II.   Three Kinds of Gifts
    III. Different Gifts, Ministries, and Workings
    IV. Ministering God's Grace
    V.   Maturity Increases Effectiveness
    VI. Overview
    VII. Summation

CONTENTS

Lesson Six   The Supportive Leadership Gifts 109
  I.   The Supportive Gifts in Christ's Body
  II.   The Gift of Apostleship
  III.   The Prophetic Gift
  IV.   The Evangelist
  V.   The Pastor-Teacher
  VI.   The Teacher
  VII.   Their Combined Task
  VIII. Summation

Lesson Seven   Motivational Gifts Part I 129
  I.   Introduction
  II.   The Motivational Gift Approach
  III.   Commentary on Romans 12:1-8
  IV.   Motivational Gifts in Action
  V.   Summation

Lesson Eight   Motivational Gifts Part II 165
  I.   The Gift of Prophecy
  II.   The Gift of Serving
  III.   The Gift of Teaching
  IV.   The Gift of Exhortation
  V.   The Gift of Giving
  VI.   The Gift of Administration
  VII.   The Gift of Mercy
  VIII. Summation

Lesson Nine   Keeping the Local Church Healthy 213
  I.   Introduction
  II.   God's Prescription for a Healthy Church
  III.   A Healthy Church Equips
  IV.   A Healthy Church Involves Every Member in Ministry
  V.   A Healthy Church Reaches Out
  VI.   Summation

     Ministry Involvement Questionnaire

INSTRUCTIONS

Lay Leadership International materials are uniquely designed to help you gain maximum benefit from your learning experience each time you study the Bible. We recommend you follow closely the procedure outlined below.

1. **LISTEN** to the short devotional teaching for each lesson on the cassette tape that is available with this course. If this is not available, encourage your pastor or group leader to have a short time of teaching before or after each discussion time.

2. **READ** thoroughly the notes provided for each lesson. Take the time to read the scripture references that are given in the notes. The majority of these references are printed to the left of the paragraph in which they are mentioned.

3. **RESEARCH** in the Scriptures. Read the home study questions provided for the lesson then look up each reference in your Bible. The questions are designed to be answered from the Scripture verses that accompany them.

4. **WRITE** your answers down in the spaces provided. There should be ample room, especially if you write in outline form. If you need more space, use an extra sheet of paper. Answers to questions with no references either entail personal sharing or else can be found in the relevant section of the notes for that lesson. The section number in the notes is given at the top left of each page of the home study guide.

5. **DISCUSS** your answers with the small group you meet with each week. We believe that the small group experience accounts for well over 50 percent of the effectiveness of LLI training. Plan to attend the cell group every week and be prepared to discuss the answers to your home study questions with other group members.

6. **CREDIT.** Lay Leadership International credit and a *Pathway 102* diploma are awarded to those who complete all course work and attend a minimum of seven cell meetings.

THE PATHWAY OF DISCIPLESHIP
MASTER DIAGRAM
MATTHEW 5:3-16

1. "Blessed are the poor in spirit."
2. "Blessed are those who mourn."
3. "Blessed are the meek."
4. "Blessed are those who hunger and thirst for righteousness."
5. "Blessed are the merciful."
6. "Blessed are the pure in heart."
7. "Blessed are the peacemakers."
8. "Blessed are those who are persecuted because of righteousness."
9. "You are the salt of the earth."
   "You are the light of the world."

9. SALT & LIGHT
8. PERSECUTION
7. PEACEMAKING
6. PURITY
5. MERCY
4. SPIRITUAL HUNGER
3. MEEKNESS
2. SPIRITUAL MOURNING
1. POVERTY OF SPIRIT

THE NEW BIRTH: THE FIRST STEP ON THE PATHWAY OF DISCIPLESHIP

101   102   103   104

A NOTE FROM THE AUTHOR

Dear friend:

In *Pathway 101 and 102* we learned that within the framework of the local church, Christ is molding us into His image. Each new beatitude demonstrates yet another aspect of His character exerting an influence upon our character as we seek to follow Him.

Pathway 103 deals with, "Blessed are the merciful" which we call the essential response of discipleship. God is love and through His church and its individual members, He seeks to bring His mercy to the world. To grow in mercy is to view the world as God does, to feel for the world as God does, and to take action in the world as God has done through Jesus Christ.

Pathway 103 will give you an expanded understanding of how we, the church, collectively bring His love to the world. It will lead you into the fascinating study of your place in the body of Christ. This will involve discovering who you are as a person, as well as evaluating your own spiritual gifts, talents, and abilities.

At the conclusion of the course, you should understand more than you ever have before how the church is called to function in both the community and the world. Hopefully, you will discover more clearly your personal role in whatever local expression of Christ's body you belong.

Many have told me that this course is like the icing on the cake. It gives them a fuller perspective on all that has been studied in the Beatitudes thus far. May *Pathway 103* enrich you and open to you a door of ministry that will bless the world with a fresh expression of God's love through your life.

Sincerely in Christ,

Rev. Donald E. Hill
President, Lay Leadership International

ABBREVIATIONS

OLD TESTAMENT

Gen.	Genesis	Eccl.	Ecclesiastes
Ex.	Exodus	Song	Song of Solomon
Lev.	Leviticus	Isa.	Isaiah
Num.	Numbers	Jer.	Jeremiah
Deut.	Deuteronomy	Lam.	Lamentations
Josh.	Joshua	Ez.	Ezekiel
Jdg.	Judges	Dan.	Daniel
Ruth	Ruth	Hos.	Hosea
I Sam.	I Samuel	Joel	Joel
II Sam.	II Samuel	Amos	Amos
I Kg.	I Kings	Obad.	Obadiah
II Kg.	II Kings	Jon.	Jonah
I Chr.	I Chronicles	Mic.	Micah
II Chr.	II Chronicles	Nah.	Nahum
Ezra	Ezra	Hab.	Habakkuk
Neh.	Nehemiah	Zeph.	Zephaniah
Est.	Esther	Hag.	Haggai
Job	Job	Zech.	Zechariah
Ps.	Psalms	Mal.	Malachi
Prov.	Proverbs		

NEW TESTAMENT

Matt.	Matthew	I Tim.	I Timothy
Mk.	Mark	II Tim.	II Timothy
Lu.	Luke	Tit.	Titus
Jn.	John	Phlem.	Philemon
Acts	Acts	Heb.	Hebrews
Ro.	Romans	Jas.	James
I Cor.	I Corinthians	I Pet.	I Peter
II Cor.	II Corinthians	II Pet.	II Peter
Gal.	Galatians	I Jn.	I John
Eph.	Ephesians	II Jn.	II John
Phil.	Philippians	III Jn.	III John
Col.	Colossians	Jude	Jude
I Thess.	I Thessalonians	Rev.	Revelation
II Thess.	II Thessalonians		

BIBLE VERSIONS

AB	The Amplified Bible
KJV	King James Version
RSV	Revised Standard Version
TLB	The Living Bible

MERCY

The Essential Response of Discipleship

LESSON ONE — BLESSED ARE THE MERCIFUL

OUTLINE

Lesson One Synopsis

I. **INTRODUCTION**

II. **WHAT IS GOD'S MERCY?**
   A. Mercy is How God Views His Creation
   B. Mercy is God's Intense Feelings About His Creation
   C. Mercy is God's Motivation to Act

III. **JESUS COMMUNICATED HIS FATHER'S HEART**
   A. Christ's Oneness With the Father
   B. Christ's Inner Feelings
   C. Christ's Emotions Motivated Him to Action

IV. **WHO ARE THE MERCIFUL?**
   A. A Work of the Spirit
   B. The Merciful View the World as God Does
   C. The Merciful Feel for the World as God Does
   D. The Merciful Take Action as God Does

V. **A PRACTICAL ILLUSTRATION OF MERCY**
   A. Keys to the Good Samaritan

VI. **SUMMATION**

Home Study Guide

"Blessed are the merciful, for they will receive mercy"
(Mt. 5:7)

Mercy is another of the key characteristics of the disciple of Jesus Christ. We are essentially called to be like Him, and since He is merciful, we should be merciful.

God is merciful. His mercy is a fundamental aspect of how He views His creation both before and after the Fall. Mercy represents God's intense feelings of pity and compassion for the situation of humanity. These feelings motivate Him to act on our behalf.

If we are to discover the nature and extent of God's mercy, we need only to look at the Lord Jesus who was and is completely one with the Father. All that the Father is, Christ is. Therefore, as we look at the mercy of Jesus Christ, we see God's mercy.

If we are to become merciful like Christ, we must allow the Holy Spirit to cultivate God's mercy within us. It can be ours in no other way. When this takes place, we will begin to view the world in mercy as God does, feel mercy and compassion for the world as God does, and act mercifully toward the world as God does. Perhaps the best practical illustration of this mercy we see in the New Testament, outside of the ministry of Jesus, is found in the Parable of the Good Samaritan.

I. INTRODUCTION

"Blessed are the merciful, for they will receive mercy."
(Mt. 5:7)

A. Mercy is one of the qualities that inevitably manifests itself in the life of every true disciple. Those who are merciful are promised that they will receive mercy. This does not mean they earn God's mercy by being merciful to others. God's mercy comes to us only through His grace.

To receive God's mercy we must repent. If we truly repent and ask God's forgiveness for ourselves, we cannot withhold mercy and forgiveness from others as the Parable of the Unforgiving Servant clearly demonstrates (Mt. 18:23-35). The result, therefore, is that those who repent and receive God's mercy, are inevitably those who are merciful to others.

B. *Pathway of Discipleship 103* concentrates on what it means for the disciple to be merciful, not only in a personal sense, but particularly with reference to God's strategy for expressing His mercy to the world through the body of Christ. In this regard we make an extensive study of the disciple's contribution to the ministry of the body of Christ by means of his spiritual gifts.

C. Refer to the Pathway of Discipleship Master Diagram found on page viii.

1. *Pathway 101 and 102* discuss the qualities of spiritual hunger, poverty of spirit, spiritual mourning, and meekness.

2. We can see that mercy is another characteristic of the maturing disciple that must be cultivated so that he can become salt and light to the world and thus bring glory to God (Mt. 5:13-16). *Pathway 103* centers on this quality of mercy.

3. *Pathway 104* discusses the qualities of purity and peacemaking, as well as the persecution which these qualities provoke. It ends by summarizing

Matthew 18:23-35

"Therefore, the kingdom of heaven is like a king who wanted to settle accounts with his servants. ²⁴As he began the settlement, a man who owed him ten thousand talents was brought to him. ²⁵Since he was not able to pay, the master ordered that he and his wife and his children and all that he had be sold to repay the debt.

²⁶"The servant fell on his knees before him. 'Be patient with me,' he begged, 'and I will pay back everything.' ²⁷The servant's master took pity on him, canceled the debt and let him go. ²⁸"But when that servant went out, he found one of his fellow servants who owed him a hundred denarii. He grabbed him and began to choke him. 'Pay back what you owe me!' he demanded.

²⁹"His fellow servant fell to his knees and begged him, 'Be patient with me, and I will pay you back.'

³⁰"But he refused. Instead, he went off and had the man thrown into prison until he could pay the debt. ³¹When the other servants saw what had happened, they were greatly distressed and went and told their master everything that had happened.

³²"Then the master called the servant in. 'You wicked servant,' he said, 'I canceled all that debt of yours because you begged me to. ³³Shouldn't you have had mercy on your fellow servant just as I had on you?' ³⁴In anger his master turned him over to the jailers until he should pay back all he owed.

³⁵"This is how my heavenly Father will treat each of you unless you forgive your brother from your heart."

Matthew 5:13-16

"You are the salt of the earth. But if the salt loses its saltiness, how can it be made salty again? It is no longer good for anything, except to be thrown out and trampled by men. ¹⁴"You are the light of the world. A city on a hill cannot be hidden. ¹⁵Neither do people light a lamp and put it under a bowl. Instead they put it on its stand, and it gives light to everyone in the house. ¹⁶In the same way, let your light shine before men, that they may see your good deeds and praise your Father in heaven.

II. WHAT IS GOD'S MERCY?

how the disciple who has reached maturity within the framework of the local church becomes salt and light to the world.

II. WHAT IS GOD'S MERCY?

Mercy is the aspect of God's love which represents:

1. How He views His fallen creation.

2. His intense feelings for the situation of fallen humanity.

3. His motivation to action. God's mercy motivates Him to do something about the human condition.

A. Mercy is How God Views His Creation

1. Before the Fall

   a. God created man totally perfect and whole. He placed him in a perfect environment that was in absolute harmony with man's being. There were no inner or outer conflicts in Adam and Eve's existence (Gen. chapters 1-2).

      (1) *Adam was spiritually in harmony.* He was joined to God. He had pure and unhindered fellowship in the Spirit.

      (2) *Adam was psychologically in harmony.* He knew no fear or evil because he walked in the holy, pure, and protected environment of Eden. His thoughts were holy, pure, positive, and in total harmony with his spirit and with God's truth.

      (3) *Adam was physically in harmony.* There was no sickness. He had eternal access to the tree of life (Gen. 2:9, 15-17).

      (4) *Adam was in harmony with his world.* There was no aggressive drive in the animal kingdom. There was no hostility in man (sociological harmony). Adam cultivated the earth with joy and ease before the Fall (Gen. 2:8-9).

Genesis 2:9, 15-17
And the LORD God made all kinds of trees grow out of the ground—trees that were pleasing to the eye and good for food. In the middle of the garden were the tree of life and the tree of the knowledge of good and evil.

[15]The LORD God took the man and put him in the Garden of Eden to work it and take care of it. [16]And the LORD God commanded the man, "You are free to eat from any tree in the garden; [17]but you must not eat from the tree of the knowledge of good and evil, for when you eat of it you will surely die."

II. WHAT IS GOD'S MERCY?

Genesis 3:16, 24
To the woman he said,

"I will greatly increase your pains in
    childbearing;
with pain you will give birth to children.
Your desire will be for your husband,
    and he will rule over you."

24 After he drove the man out, he placed on the
east side of the Garden of Eden cherubim and
a flaming sword flashing back and forth to
guard the way to the tree of life.

Genesis 3:8
Then the man and his wife heard the sound of
the LORD God as he was walking in the garden
in the cool of the day, and they hid from the
LORD God among the trees of the garden.

Genesis 3:14
So the LORD God said to the serpent, "Because you have done this,

"Cursed are you above all the livestock
    and all the wild animals!
You will crawl on your belly
    and you will eat dust
    all the days of your life.

Genesis 3:21
The LORD God made garments of skin for
Adam and his wife and clothed them.

Genesis 4:14-15
Today you are driving me from the land, and
I will be hidden from your presence; I will be a
restless wanderer on the earth, and whoever
finds me will kill me."
15 But the LORD said to him, "Not so, if anyone kills Cain, he will suffer vengeance seven
times over." Then the LORD put a mark on Cain
so that no one who found him would kill him.

Genesis 8:22
"As long as the earth endures,
seedtime and harvest,
cold and heat,
summer and winter,
day and night
will never cease."

Genesis 12:1-3
The LORD had said to Abram, "Leave your
country, your people and your father's household and go to the land I will show you.

2 "I will make you into a great nation
    and I will bless you;
I will make your name great,
    and you will be a blessing.
3 I will bless those who bless you,
    and whoever curses you I will curse;
and all peoples on earth
    will be blessed through you."

b. This perfect start for mankind came as a result of
God's grace. Adam and Eve were placed in a
world that was totally suited to their needs.

2. After the Fall

a. Sin brought total disharmony to man's world.

(1) Physical disharmony (Gen. 3:16, 24).

(2) Spiritual disharmony (Gen. 3:8).

(3) Disharmony in the animal kingdom (Gen.
3:14).

(4) Disharmony in the earth (Gen. 3:17-19).

(5) Social disharmony (Gen. 4:8).

b. Despite the devastation and disharmony that
resulted from the Fall, God's basic attitude toward His creation still remained merciful. This is
clearly demonstrated by the following facts:

(1) God provided a covering for Adam and Eve
after they had sinned (Gen. 3:21).

(2) God even showed mercy on Cain, the first
murderer and gave him a sign to protect him
from other men even though he had to wander
the earth as an outcast (Gen. 4:14-15).

(3) God continued to sustain the earth physically, providing sunshine, moisture, and so
forth, even though it suffered the effects of
the Fall (Gen. 8:22).

(4) God took steps to redeem man from his fallen
condition by calling Abraham and forming
the nation of Israel through which He would
reveal His law and eventually send His Son,
Jesus Christ, as the final solution to the fall of
man (Gen. 12:1-3).

LESSON ONE · BLESSED ARE THE MERCIFUL

II. WHAT IS GOD'S MERCY?

B. Mercy is God's Intense Feelings About His Creation

Because of His love, God feels an extreme sense of pity and compassion for the plight of His creation.

1. God's Pity

    a. God created man perfect in His image in a perfect environment, a world in complete harmony with Himself.

    b. His love now looks with *pity* upon that creation that is so far from Eden's glory, a humanity out of harmony with itself, its environment, and its Creator.

2. God's Compassion

    This aspect of God's nature is most fully expressed in the feelings of His Son. These feelings are described throughout the Gospels (see Section III, B, Christ's Inner Feelings).

C. Mercy is God's Motivation to Act

1. God's mercy is His primary motivation.

    a. It is God's feeling of mercy toward His creation that motivates Him to take action.

    b. God's mercy motivated Him to send Jesus Christ:

    > God has told us his secret reason for sending Christ, a plan he decided on *in mercy* long ago; and this was his purpose: that when the time is ripe he will gather us all together from wherever we are—in heaven or on earth—to be with him in Christ, forever.
    > (Eph. 1:9-10, TLB, emphasis added)

    c. God's mercy motivates Him to inspire men to continue the demonstration and proclamation of His message of redemption and restoration for all mankind.

III. JESUS COMMUNICATED HIS FATHER'S HEART

Ephesians 1:9-10
And he made known to us the mystery of his will according to his good pleasure, which he purposed in Christ, [10] to be put into effect when the times will have reached their fulfillment— to bring all things in heaven and on earth together under one head, even Christ.

2. God's love is infinite. His mercy extends far beyond simple feelings of pity. God's love and mercy will go to the furthest degree to restore man to what He originally intended him to be.

3. *God's desire is to bring total restoration to man's condition.* The good news of the gospel is that God provides a way, through Jesus Christ, for His creation to be ultimately restored (Eph. 1:9-10).

III. JESUS COMMUNICATED HIS FATHER'S HEART

More than anything else, the Person of Jesus Christ reveals the Father's love, mercy, and compassion for His creation.

A. Christ's Oneness With the Father

1. Jesus Christ revealed Himself as being all the Father wanted to be to His creation. "The words I say to you are not just my own. Rather, it is the Father, living in me, who is doing his work" (Jn. 14:10).

2. Every word of Christ, every action, every miracle explicitly and fully demonstrated God's burning desire for His creation. (This thought is expanded on in Lesson 2).

B. Christ's Inner Feelings

1. If Jesus Christ revealed all the Father was, then *the scriptural portrayal of Christ's inner feelings toward suffering humanity fully expresses the Father's heart of pity and compassion.*

Matthew 9:35-38 (KJV)
And Jesus went about all the cities and villages, teaching in their synagogues, and preaching the gospel of the kingdom, and healing every sickness and every disease among the people. [36] But when he saw the multitudes, he was moved with compassion on them, because they fainted, and were scattered abroad, as sheep having no shepherd. [37] Then saith he unto his disciples, The harvest truly is plenteous, but the labourers are few; [38] Pray ye therefore the Lord of the harvest, that he will send forth labourers into his harvest.

2. No portion of Scripture more fully expresses the emotional feelings of Jesus Christ than Matthew 9:35-38.

a. Verse 36 says Christ was "moved with compassion." This is the strongest word for pity in the Greek language. It actually conveys that Jesus was moved to the depths of His bowels. The word

III. JESUS COMMUNICATED HIS FATHER'S HEART

Matthew 14:14
When Jesus landed and saw a large crowd, he had compassion on them and healed their sick.

Matthew 20:34
Jesus had compassion on them and touched their eyes. Immediately they received their sight and followed him.

Mark 9:20-27
So they brought him. When the spirit saw Jesus, it immediately threw the boy into a convulsion. He fell to the ground and rolled around, foaming at the mouth.
²¹ Jesus asked the boy's father, "How long has he been like this?"
"From childhood," he answered. ²² "It has often thrown him into fire or water to kill him. But if you can do anything, take pity on us and help us."
²³ "'If you can'?" said Jesus. "Everything is possible for him who believes."
²⁴ Immediately the boy's father exclaimed, "I do believe; help me overcome my unbelief!"
²⁵ When Jesus saw that a crowd was running to the scene, he rebuked the evil spirit. "You deaf and dumb spirit," he said, "I command you, come out of him and never enter him again."
²⁶ The spirit shrieked, convulsed him violently and came out. The boy looked so much like a corpse that many said "He's dead." ²⁷ But Jesus took him by the hand and lifted him to his feet, and he stood up.

Luke 7:12-13
As he approached the town gate, a dead person was being carried out—the only son of his mother, and she was a widow. And a large crowd from the town was with her. ¹³ When the Lord saw her, his heart went out to her and he said, "Don't cry."

Matthew 15:32
Jesus called his disciples to him and said, "I have compassion for these people; they have already been with me three days and have nothing to eat. I do not want to send them away hungry, or they may collapse on the way."

describes a man moved to the depths of his entire being with a burdening emotion.

b. William Barclay points out that in the Gospels, apart from some of the parables, this expression "moved with compassion" is used only pertaining to Jesus Christ.

C. Christ's Emotions Motivated Him to Action

1. Everywhere Jesus went He was doing good. Both His words and His miracles revealed how God the Father felt and what He wanted to do for His creation.

2. Throughout the Gospels, Christ is depicted in at least five different ways as having the same kind of deep compassion spoken of in Matthew 9:36. Each time He is moved with a deep pity that motivates Him to take action to relieve a situation of human suffering:

   a. Christ was moved with compassion for the physically infirmed:

      (1) The sick (Mt. 14:14).
      (2) The blind (Mt. 20:34).
      (3) The demonized (Mk. 9:20-27).

      Christ could not see human pain without being moved to ease it.

   b. Christ was moved with compassion for people experiencing deep sorrow:

      The widow of Nain (Lk. 7:12-13).

   c. Christ was moved with compassion for the hungry:

      He felt deep pity for those who had gone without food for three days (Mt. 15:32).

   d. Christ was moved with compassion for the lonely and alienated:

      Nothing can be more devastating than social ostracism, yet the leper was sentenced to such a

IV. WHO ARE THE MERCIFUL?

Mark 1:40-42
A man with leprosy came to him and begged him on his knees, "If you are willing, you can make me clean."
[41] Filled with compassion, Jesus reached out his hand and touched the man. "I am willing," he said. "Be clean!" [42] Immediately the leprosy left him and he was cured.

life. When confronted with this, Jesus was moved with deep compassion (Mk. 1:40-42).

e. Christ was moved with compassion for the spiritually bewildered. Jesus describes the spiritual condition of mankind in Matthew 9:36. The thought translated from the original Greek portrays helpless men like bewildered sheep. The Greek word used describes someone who has been harassed without pity and treated badly until they are weary with exhaustion. As a result they have thrown themselves down and now lie helpless.

3. In each of the five areas described above (a-e), Jesus took action. His compassion always compelled Him to lift men out of sorrowful situations.

4. Jesus Christ revealed a wholistic concern for man's condition. He was concerned with the needs of the whole person: body, soul, and spirit. He did more than meet man's spiritual needs. Every human need (physical, social, psychological, and spiritual) moved Him with great pity. Christians must be the same. Although the spiritual is of ultimate importance, we cannot consider man as only a soul that needs to be saved.

5. The love of God motivates us to compassionate action in every human circumstance. People who are only motivated to meet spiritual needs misunderstand God's concern for man's fallen condition in all of its aspects. Although spiritual regeneration must be our first concern, it is not the only concern. Evangelism must be wholistic in its approach to human need. It must reach out to the whole person. The love of God demands that we feed the hungry, heal the sick, set free the oppressed, as well as preach the gospel.

IV. WHO ARE THE MERCIFUL?

The merciful, through the inner renewing work of the Holy Spirit:

IV. WHO ARE THE MERCIFUL?

1. View the world as God does.
2. Feel for the world as God does.
3. Are motivated to action as God was in Jesus Christ.

A. A Work of the Spirit

1. To view the world, to feel for the world, and to take action for the world as God does, is a result of His inner renewing work. It is the result of grace.

2. This kind of mercy must spring from a love that is beyond human ability. It has to be more than simply a humanitarian outlook on life. It must be the result of yielding to the Spirit's desire within or it is not truly God's mercy that is demonstrated.

3. In *Pathway 101*, Lesson 7, Section III, C, five reasons were cited for trials and testings in our lives. The last reason was to help those who minister have empathy in certain areas of their lives.

   a. God's Spirit works in all things to help us feel for the hurts of humanity:

   2 Corinthians 1:6-7 (TLB)
   We are in deep trouble for bringing you God's comfort and salvation. But in our trouble God had comforted us—and this, too, to help you: to show you from our personal experience how God will tenderly comfort you when you undergo these same sufferings. He will give you the strength to endure.

   (1) Paul's example (2 Cor. 1:6-7).

   (2) Quite often, people with great healing ministries have been raised from a death bed or a prolonged struggle with sickness.

   (3) God can use our past financial struggles or struggles of any kind to help us more effectively minister in love and understanding to others.

   (4) This does not mean we cannot empathize and effectively minister without experiencing past struggles. However, God can and does use our struggles to help us feel more deeply the hurts of others.

   Hebrews 2:10
   In bringing many sons to glory, it was fitting that God, for whom and through whom everything exists, should make the author of their salvation perfect through suffering.

   b. Christ is our example in showing us the value of suffering. He suffered so that God might understand the frailties of man (Heb. 2:10).

IV. WHO ARE THE MERCIFUL?

Genesis 3:14-19
So the LORD God said to the serpent, "Because you have done this,

"Cursed are you above all the
    livestock
  and all the wild animals!
You will crawl on your belly
  and you will eat dust
  all the days of your life.
[15] And I will put enmity
  between you and the woman,
  and between your offspring and hers;
he will crush your head,
  and you will strike his heel."
[16] To the woman he said,

"I will greatly increase your pains in
  childbearing;
  with pain you will give birth to children.
Your desire will be for your husband,
  and he will rule over you."

[17] To Adam he said, "Because you listened to your wife and ate from the tree about which I commanded you, 'You must not eat of it,'

"Cursed is the ground because of you;
  through painful toil you will eat of it
  all the days of your life.
[18] It will produce thorns and thistles for you,
  and you will eat the plants of the field.
[19] By the sweat of your brow
  you will eat your food
until you return to the ground,
  since from it you were taken;
for dust you are
  and to dust you will return."

Romans 8:22-23
We know that the whole creation has been groaning as in the pains of childbirth right up to the present time. [23] Not only so, but we ourselves, who have the firstfruits of the Spirit, groan inwardly as we wait eagerly for our adoption as sons, the redemption of our bodies.

Hebrews 4:15
For we do not have a high priest who is unable to sympathize with our weaknesses, but we have one who has been tempted in every way, just as we are—yet was without sin.

B. The Merciful View the World as God Does

1. The merciful fully accept the biblical description of the human condition.

2. The world is totally marred by the Fall. Every aspect of man's physical, mental, and social environment is suffering. Everyone in some way is sick and out of harmony with God (Gen. 3:14-19).

3. Romans 8:22-23 vividly illustrates this condition:

> For we know that even the things of nature, like animals and plants, suffer in sickness and death as they await this great event. And even we Christians, although we have the Holy Spirit within us as a foretaste of future glory, also groan to be released from pain and suffering. We, too, wait anxiously for that day when God will give us our full rights as his children, including the new bodies he has promised us—bodies that will never be sick again and will never die (TLB).

C. The Merciful Feel for the World as God Does

1. This is usually an outgrowth of our prayer life and relationship to Jesus Christ.

  a. Reese Howells, the great British prayer warrior, gives the following threefold outline of intercession as he experienced it.[1]

    (1) Identification

    Jesus identified with sinful man. He felt as we feel. The intercessor feels the hurts and is sensitive to the results of sinful living in those for whom he prays. Because Jesus was touched with the feelings of our infirmities, He can be an effective intercessor for us in heaven (Heb. 4:15).

    (2) Agony

    In Nehemiah, chapter 1, we see the emotional agony this man of God experienced as he

---

[1] Norman Grubb, *Reese Howells Intercessor* (Lutterworth Press, 1973), pp. 86-91.

IV. WHO ARE THE MERCIFUL?

Nehemiah 1:1-11
The words of Nehemiah son of Hacaliah:

In the month of Kislev in the twentieth year, while I was in the citadel of Susa, [2]Hanani, one of my brothers, came from Judah with some other men, and I questioned them about the Jewish remnant that survived the exile, and also about Jerusalem. [3]They said to me, "Those who survived the exile and are back in the province are in great trouble and disgrace. The wall of Jerusalem is broken down, and its gates have been burned with fire."
[4]When I heard these things, I sat down and wept. For some days I mourned and fasted and prayed before the God of heaven.[5]Then I said:

"O LORD, God of heaven, the great and awesome God, who keeps his covenant of love with those who love him and obey his commands, [6]let your ear be attentive and your eyes open to hear the prayer your servant is praying before you day and night for your servants, the people of Israel. I confess the sins we Israelites, including myself and my father's house, have committed against you. [7]We acted very wickedly toward you. We have not obeyed the commands, decrees and laws you gave your servant Moses.
[8]"Remember the instruction you gave your servant Moses, saying, 'If you are unfaithful, I will scatter you among the nations, [9]but if you return to me and obey my commands, then even if your exiled people are at the farthest horizon, I will gather them from there and bring them to the place I have chosen as a dwelling for my Name.'
[10]"They are your servants and your people, whom you redeemed by your great strength and your mighty hand. [11]O Lord, let your ear be attentive to the prayer of this your servant and to the prayer of your servants who delight in revering your name. Give your servant success today by granting him favor in the presence of this man."

I was cupbearer to the king.

Hebrews 4:15-16
For we do not have a high priest who is unable to sympathize with our weaknesses, but we have one who has been tempted in every way, just as we are—yet was without sin. [16]Let us then approach the throne of grace with confidence, so that we may receive mercy and find grace to help us in our time of need.

James 2:14-17 (TLB)
Dear brothers, what's the use of saying that you have faith and are Christians, if you aren't proving it by helping others? Will that kind of faith save anyone? If you have a friend who is in need of food and clothing, and you say to him, "Well, good-bye and God bless you; stay

interceded on behalf of Jerusalem (Neh. 1:1-11). Deep intercession causes us times of emotional agony as we mourn the devastating results of sin in people's lives.

(3) Authority

Reese Howells said, "*If the intercessor knows identification and agony, he also knows authority.*"[2] This is prayer in perfect harmony with the will of the Father. With it comes a special faith which drives back every border of Satan's kingdom. Often one has to pray through the agony of a burden until God's gift of faith is received and Christ's power is released, resulting in great victory.

2. Feeling for the world as God does is like suffering with Jesus Christ. This fellowship in Christ's sufferings is one of three aspects of discipleship Paul emphasizes in Philippians 3:10. Christ calls each one to share with Him in the fellowship of His sufferings (see *Pathway 101*, Lesson 2). Christ is an intercessor today and is asking His body to enter into that same intercession (Heb. 4:15-16). He is asking His Church to feel for the hurts of humanity as He does.

3. The merciful are disciples who, through a renewed mind and a diligent prayer life, feel the heart of Jesus Christ as He felt the heart of the Father:

> When He saw the throngs, He was moved with pity and sympathy for them, because they were bewildered—harassed and distressed and dejected and helpless—like sheep without a shepherd.
>
> (Mt. 9:36, AB)

D. The Merciful Take Action as God Does

1. Action proves whether or not a person's faith is genuine (Jas. 2:14-17).

2. The merciful always take action for those who cannot help themselves.

---

[2]*Reese Howells Intercessor*, emphasis added, p. 89.

IV. WHO ARE THE MERCIFUL?

warm and eat hearty," and then don't give him clothes or food, what good does that do? So you see, it isn't enough just to have faith. You must also do good to prove that you have it. Faith that doesn't show itself by good works is no faith at all—it is dead and useless.

Mark 14:65
Then some began to spit at him; they blindfolded him, struck him with their fists, and said, "Prophesy!" And the guards took him and beat him.

Mark 15:16-20
The soldiers led Jesus away into the palace (that is, the Praetorium) and called together the whole company of soldiers. [17] They put a purple robe on him, then wove a crown of thorns and set it on him. [18] And they began to call out to him, "Hail, King of the Jews!" [19] Again and again they struck him on the head with a staff and spit on him. Falling on their knees, they worshiped him. [20] And when they had mocked him, they took off the purple robe and put his own clothes on him. Then they led him out to crucify him.

Isaiah 53:7
He was oppressed and afflicted,
  yet he did not open his mouth;
he was led like a lamb to the
    slaughter,
and as a sheep before her shearers
    is silent,
so he did not open his mouth.

Romans 5:6-8
You see, at just the right time, when we were still powerless, Christ died for the ungodly. [7] Very rarely will anyone die for a righteous man, though for a good man someone might possibly dare to die. [8] But God demonstrates his own love for us in this: While we were still sinners, Christ died for us.

a. This requires loving as God loves—with no strings attached.

  (1) "In this act we see what real love is: it is not our love for God, but his love for us when he sent his Son to satisfy God's anger against our sins" (I John 4:10, TLB).

  (2) The love described above is closely related to the quality of meekness (see *Pathway 102*). It is a love that loves without being loved. It is a love that chooses to claim no personal rights in order that the other person may be saved.

  (3) Jesus Christ exhibited this love when He was beaten and spit upon, yet He opened not His mouth (Mk. 14:65, 15:16-20; Isa. 53:7).

b. Romans 5:6-8 shows that God extends His love to all men regardless of the anticipated response. The character of God is such that His mercy continues regardless of man's rejection. "The Lord is not slack concerning his promise, . . . but is longsuffering to us-ward, not willing that any should perish, but that all should come to repentance" (2 Pet. 3:9, KJV).

c. The merciful Christian loves with no ulterior motives. He chooses to love with no strings attached. His love is not a form of coercion. Love is not to be given with the ulterior motive that unless a person comes to Christ, his caring will be withdrawn. His highest desire is to see that a person is genuinely converted. God's love in action always says, "No matter if you respond to Christ or not, I will help you and be merciful to you because God loves you and so do I."

d. Mercy is showing God's pity and compassion for people who are totally unable to help themselves:

  "Mercy is a form of love determined by the state or condition of its objects. Their state is one of suffering and need, while they may be unworthy or ill-deserving. Mercy is . . . the kindly ministry

V. A PRACTICAL ILLUSTRATION OF MERCY

of love for their relief.'' (Miley, Syst. Theol., i, 209, 210). The expression "I will have mercy, and not sacrifice" indicates that God is pleased with the exercise of mercy rather than with the offering of sacrifices, . . . Mercy is a Christian grace, and is strongly urged toward all men (Mt. 5:7, 23:23; Jas. 3:17, etc.).''[3]

V. A PRACTICAL ILLUSTRATION OF MERCY

The practical implications of what it means to be merciful are clearly portrayed in the Parable of the Good Samaritan.

A. Keys to the Good Samaritan (Lk. 10:25-37)

1. Loving God is synonymous with loving your neighbor. You cannot love one without loving the other.

2. The lawyer who asked the question, "Who is my neighbor," portrays the attitude of the nominal Christian: "Of course I'm willing to love my neighbor, but the reason I'm not doing it, is that I really don't know who my neighbor is." The nominal Christian knows he should be loving his neighbor but is not doing so and thus seeks an excuse to justify his disobedience. The real problem is, unless a person is born again and walking in the Spirit, he lacks the God-given motivation to be merciful.

3. The priest portrays an attitude often found in the Christian church; a type of self-righteous snobbery, that it is somehow unspiritual to dirty one's hands in the world. These same people criticized Jesus for being among publicans and sinners.

4. The scribe, or temple assistant, portrays a man who takes time to observe, but who is so wrapped up in the schedule of his own life and the life of the church, that he has no time to help. Jesus put people first. The Good Samaritan dropped everything to help. This is God's desire.

Luke 10:25-37

On one occasion an expert in the law stood up to test Jesus. "Teacher," he asked, "what must I do to inherit eternal life?"
[26]"What is written in the Law?" he replied. "How do you read it?"
[27]He answered: "'Love the Lord your God with all your heart and with all your soul and with all your strength and with all your mind'; and, 'Love your neighbor as yourself.'"
[28]"You have answered correctly," Jesus replied. "Do this and you will live."
[29]But he wanted to justify himself, so he asked Jesus, "And who is my neighbor?"
[30]In reply Jesus said: "A man was going down from Jerusalem to Jericho, when he fell into the hands of robbers. They stripped him of his clothes, beat him and went away, leaving him half dead. [31]A priest happened to be going down the same road, and when he saw the man, he passed by on the other side. [32]So too, a Levite, when he came to the place and saw him, passed by on the other side. [33]But a Samaritan, as he traveled, came where the man was; and when he saw him, he took pity on him. [34]He went to him and bandaged his wounds, pouring on oil and wine. Then he put the man on his own donkey, took him to an inn and took care of him. [35]The next day he took out two silver coins and gave them to the innkeeper. 'Look after him,' he said, 'and when I return, I will reimburse you for any extra expense you may have.'
[36]"Which of these three do you think was a neighbor to the man who fell into the hands of robbers?"
[37]The expert in the law replied, "The one who had mercy on him."
Jesus told him, "Go and do likewise."

[3] Merrill F. Unger, *Unger's Bible Dictionary* (Moody Press, 1966), p. 713.

Romans 5:10
For if, when we were God's enemies, we were reconciled to him through the death of his Son, how much more, having been reconciled, shall we be saved through his life!

5. The Good Samaritan represents one who has grasped the true implications of the Sermon on the Mount. The Samaritans hated the Jews, and vice versa. They were arch enemies, yet this man chose to love even his enemies.

6. Matthew 5:48 says that we should be perfect as our heavenly Father is perfect. The Good Samaritan chose to show love and mercy to his greatest enemy. God has done the same (Ro. 5:10).

7. Notice that the Good Samaritan was interested in ministering to the total man. He ministered to the physical need, providing first aid, transportation, food, and lodging at his own expense.

VI. SUMMATION

1. Mercy represents the way in which God views His creation both before as well as after the Fall.

2. God's mercy represents His intense feelings of pity and compassion for the plight of His fallen creation. These feelings motivated Him to take decisive action by sending Jesus Christ to heal and restore mankind.

3. Because He was fully one with the Father, Jesus Christ revealed the Father's love and compassion for this world. Christ's intense inner feelings of mercy also motivated Him to take action to heal human suffering at all levels.

4. The merciful are those who view the world as God does, who feel for the world as God does, and who are motivated to merciful activity as God was in Christ, all because of the renewing work of the Holy Spirit in their hearts.

5. The merciful are those who act to heal the whole man (body, soul and spirit), following the example of the Good Samaritan.

home study guide

LESSON ONE · DAY ONE

SECTION II

1. What is most striking about the scope and depth of God's mercy that you see in the following verses? Ps. 103:17, 106:1, 108:4; Lam. 3:22-23

_____

_____

_____

_____

2. Write a definition of God's mercy in your own words. The following verses will be helpful in formulating your answer: Joel 2:13; Mic. 7:18-19; Eph. 2:4-6; Tit. 3:5.

_____

_____

_____

_____

_____

3. a. In your own words, contrast Adam's condition before and after the Fall. Draw your information from the notes and Genesis chapters 1-4.

_____

_____

_____

_____

_____

_____

_____

b. How can we see God's mercy at work both before and after the Fall?

_____

_____

_____

_____

_____

_____

_____

home study guide

LESSON ONE · DAY TWO

SECTION III

1. Jesus Christ was one with the Father. How does this fact help us to understand the nature of God's mercy?

_____

_____

2. Why is it correct to say that Jesus' concern for people was wholistic in nature?

_____

_____

3. Study Matthew 9:36-38 and answer the following questions:
   a. Meditate upon Jesus' description of mankind in v. 36, "harassed and helpless like sheep without a shepherd." Describe how this image portrays men in modern society.

   _____

   _____

   b. In your own words, distinguish between humanitarianism or human sympathy for the condition of people and the kind of compassion expressed in the life of Jesus Christ.

   _____

   _____

   _____

   c. Do you think this kind of compassion for people is possible without the work of the Holy Spirit? Please explain your answer in light of the distinction made in part (b).

   _____

   _____

   _____

   d. In vv. 37-38 what was the chief concern of Jesus Christ regarding the multitudes? (Also see John 4:35-38.)

   _____

   _____

   e. What is your responsibility in light of the problem mentioned in v. 37?

   _____

4. In your prayer time today ask the Lord to help you see the world as He sees it. Reread Section III in the notes and be ready to share with your group on a personal level how you view the world and people. Has understanding the concept of mercy changed your attitude toward certain people?

_____

_____

Pathway of Discipleship

home study guide

LESSON ONE · DAY THREE

SECTIONS III · IV

1. In the life and ministry of Jesus Christ we see Him ministering to people on not only the spiritual level, but the psychological and physical levels as well. Please look up the following scriptures relating to the life and ministry of Jesus Christ. In each case determine whether Jesus ministered to the physical, spiritual, psychological, or social needs of mankind.

   a. Mt. 14:15-21 _____

   b. Mk. 2:1-12 _____

   c. Mk. 5:1-19 _____

   d. Lk. 8:1-3 _____

   e. Jn. 8:3-11 _____

   f. Jn. 13:4-17 _____

2. Read Acts 6:1-7, James 1:27, and Acts 2:45. What was the attitude of the early church toward taking care of those with needs within the body of Christ? What does this have to do with the concept of mercy and how should it speak to us in the modern church?

   _____

   _____

   _____

3. What areas do you see in your own church that need attention in regard to caring for people who have needs?

   _____

   _____

4. Please read Matthew 25:35-40. Analyze verse 40. What did Jesus mean by the statement "I tell you the truth, whatever you did for one of the least of these brothers of mine, you did for me."?

   _____

   _____

5. What new understanding have you gained from this week's study regarding the total implications of the gospel of Jesus Christ? How can this help us in our personal approach to people? Is evangelism simply talking to people about the Lord, or something more?

   _____

   _____

   _____

   _____

103

home study guide

LESSON ONE · DAY FOUR

SECTION IV

1. The following are incidents in Scripture where one person did not show mercy to another. In each case, what seems to be God's message to such individuals?

   a. Those who show no mercy in forgiving others. Mt. 18:21-35 _____

   _____

   _____

   b. Those who show no mercy in spirit. Ro. 1:18, 31 _____

   _____

   _____

   c. Those who show no mercy in judgment. Jas. 2:13 _____

   _____

   _____

2. Read Proverbs 3:3 and Luke 6:27-36. State in your own words what you think it means to be merciful.

   _____

   _____

   _____

3. Describe what it means to:
   a. View the world as God does. Ro. 8:22-23 _____

   _____

   _____

   _____

   b. Feel for the world as God does. Mt. 9:36 _____

   _____

   _____

   _____

   c. Take action as God does. Jas. 2:14-18 _____

   _____

   _____

   _____

4. How do our past struggles help us minister to the sufferings of others? 2 Cor. 3:3-7

   _____

   _____

Pathway of Discipleship

home study guide

LESSON ONE · DAY FIVE

SECTION V

1. Today read the Parable of the Good Samaritan in Luke 10:25-37.

2. Read the notes regarding the Good Samaritan in Section V. Describe some modern parallels of the people in the parable.

   a. People who have the attitude of the lawyer. _____
   _____
   _____
   _____

   b. People who have the attitude of the priest or the scribe. _____
   _____
   _____
   _____

   c. People who have the attitude of the Good Samaritan. _____
   _____
   _____
   _____

3. What does the story of the Good Samaritan have to do with the gospel of Jesus Christ? (This question is *not* asking you to spiritualize this parable.) _____
   _____
   _____
   _____

4. Read Luke 10:27, 36-37. State in your own words what it means to be merciful to your neighbor. _____
   _____
   _____

5. Answer this question for yourself: Who is my neighbor?_____
   _____

6. In what ways have Christians been too narrow in their understanding of evangelism and the total implications of the gospel of Jesus Christ?_____
   _____
   _____
   _____
   _____

LESSON TWO · JESUS CHRIST: GOD'S MERCY IN ACTION

OUTLINE

Lesson Two Update

Lesson Two Synopsis

I. INTRODUCTION
  A. Diagram: The Cycle of God's Mercy
  B. Diagram Explanation
  C. This Lesson

II. WHO WAS JESUS CHRIST?
  A. He Was God's Love in Action
  B. He Was God
  C. He Was the Word
  D. He Was the Word Become Flesh
  E. He Was the Creator
  F. He Was Life
  G. His Life Was the Light Men Needed

III. WHY DID JESUS CHRIST COME?
  A. To Bring God's Re-creative Life to Mankind
  B. To Reveal God and His Ways to Men

IV. HOW DID CHRIST ACCOMPLISH HIS PURPOSE?
  A. Christ Identified with the Human Condition
  B. Christ Experienced the Full Effect of Man's Sin
  C. Christ Became the Perfect Sacrifice for Man
  D. Christ Carried Away Man's Sin Forever
  E. Christ Rose from the Dead
  F. Conclusion

V. SUMMATION

Home Study Guide

LESSON TWO · JESUS CHRIST: GOD'S MERCY IN ACTION

LESSON TWO UPDATE

Lesson One

Lesson 1 began by defining God's mercy and then showing how it was demonstrated to the world in the coming of Jesus Christ. The merciful were defined as those who view the world as God does, and who take action in the world as God does. As the Parable of the Good Samaritan illustrates, mercy must be extended to the needs of the whole person—spiritual, social, and psychological.

LESSON TWO · JESUS CHRIST: GOD'S MERCY IN ACTION

LESSON TWO SYNOPSIS

Jesus Christ, His person and ministry are central to our understanding of God's mercy for His fallen creation. Christ came as the most perfect and complete expression of God's mercy to the world. Through His ministry, His death, and His resurrection, God began a great work of restoration in creation that will only be completed at Christ's return.

In every way conceivable, Christ was the perfect expression of the life, light, and love of God. He came as God's Word in human flesh to bring God's re-creative and restorative life to a world which needed it desperately. Christ came to bring this divine life to men as well as to reveal to men the character and ways of God.

Christ accomplished His purpose by means of a costly identification with the condition of fallen humanity. He took upon Himself all the limitations of human nature. He also personally experienced the full weight of God's judgment upon human sin, becoming the perfect sacrifice for man's sin which He carried away forever. In His glorious resurrection He provided the basis for man's full justification in the sight of God, and the full restoration of fellowship between God and men that was intended from the beginning.

I. INTRODUCTION

A. Diagram: The Cycle of God's Mercy

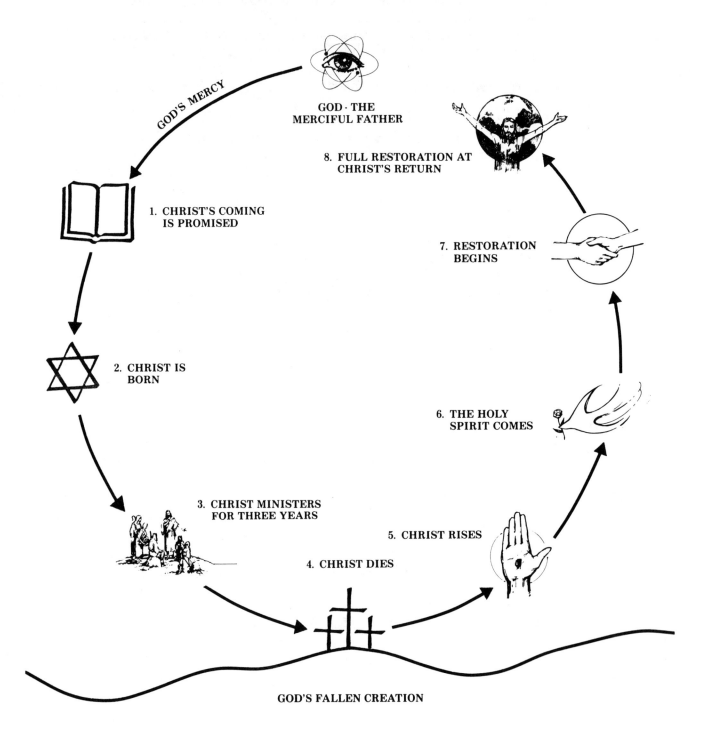

GOD · THE
MERCIFUL FATHER

GOD'S MERCY

8. FULL RESTORATION AT
CHRIST'S RETURN

1. CHRIST'S COMING
IS PROMISED

7. RESTORATION
BEGINS

2. CHRIST IS
BORN

6. THE HOLY
SPIRIT COMES

3. CHRIST MINISTERS
FOR THREE YEARS

5. CHRIST RISES

4. CHRIST DIES

GOD'S FALLEN CREATION

28

LESSON TWO · JESUS CHRIST: GOD'S MERCY IN ACTION

I. INTRODUCTION

B. Diagram Explanation

The diagram at the left shows the full cycle of God's mercy and the way in which He has expressed that mercy in the world through His Son, Jesus Christ. It depicts not only the merciful ministry of Christ Himself, but also the continuation of that ministry through the Church and the time of final restoration at Christ's return.

1. The ultimate expression of God's mercy is His sending Christ into our fallen world. This began with the promises of the coming Messiah contained in the Old Testament.

2. Christ is born at Bethlehem. He takes on humanity so that He might redeem and heal humanity.

3. Christ ministers God's Word and life to man for three years, demonstrating through His miracles the full restoration to come.

4. Christ dies on the cross for our sin. This sacrifice expresses in the most graphic way God's intense desire to redeem and restore His fallen creation.

5. Christ rises triumphant over death proving that His sacrifice for sin had been accepted by the Father as sufficient ground for our complete justification.

6. Christ sends the Holy Spirit upon the Church on the Day of Pentecost thus equipping her to carry on His ministry on earth. He has ascended to sit in the position of all power and authority at the Father's right hand. In heaven, Christ continually intercedes for the Church as she carries out her mission of bringing God's message of reconciliation to mankind.

7. The Church as Christ's body on earth begins the great work of restoring fallen mankind through the proclamation and demonstration of the gospel.

8. One day Christ will return with great power and glory to defeat His foes and establish His kingdom fully and openly throughout all the earth. At this time, the work of restoring mankind and creation from the effects of the Fall will be completed.

LESSON TWO · JESUS CHRIST: GOD'S MERCY IN ACTION

II. WHO WAS JESUS CHRIST?

I John 4:10
This is love: not that we loved God, but that he loved us and sent his Son as an atoning sacrifice for our sins.

John 14:6
Jesus answered, "I am the way and the truth and the life. No one comes to the Father except through me."

Romans 12:2
Do not conform any longer to the pattern of this world, but be transformed by the renewing of your mind. Then you will be able to test and approve what God's will is—his good, pleasing and perfect will.

James 5:14-15
Is any one of you sick? He should call the elders of the church to pray over him and anoint him with oil in the name of the Lord. [15] And the prayer offered in faith will make the sick person well; the Lord will raise him up. If he has sinned, he will be forgiven.

John 13:34-35
"A new commandment I give you: Love one another. As I have loved you, so you must love one another. [35] All men will know that you are my disciples if you love one another."

Romans 5:1-2
Therefore, since we have been justified through faith, we have peace with God through our Lord Jesus Christ, [2] through whom we have gained access by faith into his grace in which we now stand. And we rejoice in the hope of the glory of God.

Philippians 4:13
I can do everything through him who gives me strength.

John 1:1-2
In the beginning was the Word, and the Word was with God, and the Word was God. [2] He was with God in the beginning.

C. This Lesson

In this lesson we will examine the person and work of God's most wonderful and complete expression of mercy to this world: Jesus Christ.

II. WHO WAS JESUS CHRIST?

A. He Was God's Love in Action (1 John 4:10)

1. God took action to lift and restore man by offering His Son on Calvary.

2. Jesus Christ is the only way to the healing of man's total condition. Only He can restore man's relationship with God and thus enable man to draw from the reservoir of divine life (Jn. 14:6).

3. This healing begins with the regeneration of the spirit of man. The resurrection power of Christ comes to dwell within the repentant sinner's heart.

4. From within, this life-giving power of God begins through faith:

   a. To restore us psychologically (Ro. 12:2).

   b. To allow us to taste a portion of physical healing (Jas. 5:14-15).

   c. To heal our social condition; i.e., our relationships (Jn. 13:34-35).

   d. To restore spiritual communication with God by giving us access into His presence and continued victory over sin (Ro. 5:1-2, 6:22).

   e. To overcome the fears and other obstacles created by our fallen environment (Phil. 4:13).

B. He Was God

1. The Bible says that Jesus Christ existed before the beginning. He always co-existed with the Father (Jn. 1:1-2).

LESSON TWO · JESUS CHRIST: GOD'S MERCY IN ACTION

II. WHO WAS JESUS CHRIST?

Philippians 2:6
Who, being in the very nature God, did not consider equality with God something to be grasped.

John 14:9
Jesus answered: "Don't you know me, Philip, even after I have been among you such a long time? Anyone who has seen me has seen the Father. How can you say, 'Show us the Father'?"

Exodus 20:3-6
"You shall have no other gods before me. 4"You shall not make for yourself an idol in the form of anything in heaven above or on the earth beneath or in the waters below. 5You shall not bow down to them or worship them; for I, the LORD your God, am a jealous God, punishing the children for the sin of the fathers to the third and fourth generation of those who hate me, 6but showing love to thousands who love me and keep my commandments."

John 1:1
In the beginning was the Word, and the Word was with God, and the Word was God.

Colossians 2:1-3, 9
I want you to know how much I am struggling for you and for those at Laodicea, and for all who have not met me personally. 2My purpose is that they may be encouraged in heart and united in love, so that they may have the full riches of complete understanding, in order that they may know the mystery of God, namely, Christ, 3in whom are hidden all the treasures of wisdom and knowledge.

For in Christ all the fullness of the Deity lives in bodily form.

Hebrews 1:1-2
In the past God spoke to our forefathers through the prophets at many times and in various ways, 2but in these last days he has spoken to us by his Son, whom he appointed heir of all things, and through whom he made the universe.

John 1:14
The Word became flesh and lived for a while among us. We have seen his glory, the glory of the one and only Son, who came from the Father, full of grace and truth.

Matthew 1:23
"The virgin will be with child and will give birth to a son, and they will call him Immanuel" —which means, "God with us."

Hebrews 2:14
Since the children have flesh and blood, he too shared in their humanity so that by his death he might destroy him who holds the power of death—that is, the devil.

John 1:3
Through him all things were made; without him nothing was made that has been made.

Colossians 1:16
For by him all things were created: things in heaven and on earth, visible and invisible,

2. He also was God by His very nature (Phil. 2:6).

3. Christ Himself said that He was one with the Father and that he who had seen Him had seen the Father (Jn. 10:30-33, 14:9).

4. In Scripture Christ is accorded the worship and praise of the heavenly throng (Rev. ch. 5). Only God is permitted to receive worship (Exod. 20:3-6).

C. He Was the Word (John 1:1)

1. Jesus Christ was the total embodiment of divine truth. In Him were hidden all the treasures of wisdom and knowledge (Col. 2:1-3, 9).

2. Jesus came to earth as God's ultimate and complete message to mankind. In everything He did, as well as everything He said, He was God's Word of truth to humanity (Heb. 1:1-2).

D. He Was the Word Become Flesh (John 1:14)

1. He was God living among men, hence one of His names is Immanuel, God with us (Mt. 1:23).

2. He was in the fullest sense, a human being (but without a sinful nature) and yet fully God at the same time (Heb. 2:14).

3. He was God come as a man ministering God's Word and life to all He came in contact with.

E. He Was the Creator

1. Nothing was made without Him (Jn. 1:3).

2. All things were not only made through Him, they were also made for His sake (Col. 1:16).

3. He is the force that sustains the creation in its existence (Col. 1:17).

103

LESSON TWO - JESUS CHRIST: GOD'S MERCY IN ACTION

III. WHY DID JESUS CHRIST COME?

whether thrones or powers or rulers or authorities; all things were created by him and for him.

Colossians 1:17
He is before all things, and in him all things hold together.

John 1:4
In him was life, and that life was the light of men.

John 11:25
Jesus said to her, "I am the resurrection and the life. He who believes in me will live, even though he dies."

John 5:21
For just as the Father raises the dead and gives them life, even so the Son gives life to whom he is pleased to give it.

John 1:4-5
In him was life, and that life was the light of men. ⁵The light shines in the darkness, but the darkness has not understood (or overcome) it.

John 8:12
When Jesus spoke again to the people, he said, "I am the light of the world. Whoever follows me will never walk in darkness, but will have the light of life."

John 6:67-68
"You do not want to leave too, do you?" Jesus asked the Twelve.
⁶⁸Simon Peter answered him, "Lord, to whom shall we go? You have the words of eternal life."

John 10:10
The thief comes only to steal and kill and destroy; I have come that they may have life, and have it to the full.

F. He Was Life (John 1:4)

1. The Greek word for life in John 1:4 means more than mere physical life. It is the life of God. It is eternal life. It contains all of God's creative healing power.

2. Jesus said: "I am the resurrection and the life." Christ Himself is the actual creative and re-creative life of God (Jn. 11:25).

3. Jesus Christ is the universal source of all true eternal life. This life flowed from Him in the beginning as it still does today (Jn. 5:21).

G. His Life Was the Light Men Needed (John 1:4-5)

1. Man is in the darkness of poverty:

   a. Spiritual poverty

   b. Physical poverty

   c. Mental poverty

   d. Social poverty

2. Although the bleak darkness surrounding man hinders him in understanding the light of Christ, the darkness can not overcome His life and light. Acceptance of the life He brings breaks through the deepest kind of darkness (Jn. 8:12).

3. Christ brought life and immortality to light through the gospel. Only He can give the gift of eternal life (Jn. 6:67-68, 10:28; 2 Tim. 1:10).

III. WHY DID JESUS CHRIST COME?

A. To Bring God's Re-creative Life to Mankind (John 10:10)

This is the message He proclaimed and this is what He demonstrated in every miracle He performed.

32

32 © 1984 by Christos Publishing Company, Inc. All rights reserved.

Pathway of Discipleship

LESSON TWO · JESUS CHRIST: GOD'S MERCY IN ACTION

III. WHY DID JESUS CHRIST COME?

Ephesians 2:1-5
As for you, you were dead in your transgressions and sins, ²in which you used to live when you followed the ways of this world and of the ruler of the kingdom of the air, the spirit who is now at work in those who are disobedient. ³All of us also lived among them at one time, gratifying the cravings of our sinful nature and following its desires and thoughts. Like the rest, we were by nature objects of wrath. ⁴But because of his great love for us, God, who is rich in mercy; ⁵made us alive with Christ even when we were dead in transgressions—it is by grace you have been saved.

Romans 8:16-17
The Spirit himself testifies with our spirit that we are God's children. ¹⁷Now if we are children, then we are heirs—heirs of God and co-heirs with Christ, if indeed we share in his sufferings in order that we may also share in his glory.

John 7:16
Jesus answered, "My teaching is not my own. It comes from him who sent me."

John 14:8-10
Philip said, "Lord, show us the Father and that will be enough for us."
⁹Jesus answered: "Don't you know me, Philip, even after I have been among you such a long time? Anyone who has seen me has seen the Father. How can you say, 'Show us the Father'? ¹⁰Don't you believe that I am in the Father, and that the Father is in me? The words I say to you are not just my own. Rather, it is the Father, living in me, who is doing his work."

1. Jesus Christ came to bring life to a world enshrouded in death. Man was suffering from spiritual as well as physical death (Eph. 2:1-5).

2. Jesus Christ came to a sin-stricken world that was out of harmony with God and with itself:

   a. *Spiritually* sin had caused a loss of communion with the Father.

   b. *Socially* sin had brought war, hatred, and unrest.

   c. *Physically* the world was suffering from sickness and disease.

   d. *Mentally* there was derangement, loneliness, and torment.

3. Christ came to restore the human race ruined by the Fall.

   a. He came, in a sense, to give back to man the blessings of Eden: dominion over the earth and much more.

   b. The much more includes Christ's own likeness and an eternal inheritance, something Adam never had (Ro. 8:16-17).

B. To Reveal God and His Ways to Men

1. Jesus said He did not come to present His own teaching, but that of the Father who had sent Him (Jn. 7:16).

2. His character displayed all the perfections of the Father's character to mankind so that He could say, "Anyone who has seen me has seen the Father" (Jn. 14:8-10).

3. The ministry of Christ most graphically revealed God's great mercy for man, not only at its climax on the cross, but through every word, every healing, every miracle. Jesus Christ was, indeed, God's mercy in action.

LESSON TWO · JESUS CHRIST: GOD'S MERCY IN ACTION

IV. HOW DID CHRIST ACCOMPLISH HIS PURPOSE?

Philippians 2:5-7
Your attitude should be the same as that of Christ Jesus:
⁶Who, being in very nature God, did not consider equality with God something to be grasped, ⁷but made himself nothing, taking the very nature of a servant, being made in human likeness.

Romans 8:34
Who is he that condemns? Christ Jesus, who died—more than that, who was raised to life—is at the right hand of God and is also interceding for us.

Hebrews 2:17
For this reason he had to be made like his brothers in every way, in order that he might become a merciful and faithful high priest in service to God, and that he might make atonement for the sins of the people.

Hebrews 4:15-16
For we do not have a high priest who is unable to sympathize with our weaknesses, but we have one who has been tempted in every way, just as we are—yet was without sin. ¹⁶Let us then approach the throne of grace with confidence, so that we may receive mercy and find grace to help us in our time of need.

Hebrews 7:26
Such a high priest meets our need—one who is holy, blameless, pure, set apart from sinners, exalted above the heavens.

Luke 2:7
And she gave birth to her firstborn, a son. She wrapped him in strips of cloth and placed him in a manger, because there was no room for them in the inn.

IV. HOW DID CHRIST ACCOMPLISH HIS PURPOSE?

A. Christ Identified with the Human Condition

1. By taking on humanity, Christ was in a position to fully identify with the human condition. Only this radical step of condescension, God becoming a man, could permit such a complete and genuine identification with man (Phil. 2:5-7).

2. Christ's total identification with human need prepared Him for His high priestly ministry in heaven today.

   a. He became man's faithful high priest interceding on man's behalf (Ro. 8:34).

   b. It was necessary for God to experience the human situation before man's case could be fully understood and argued in heaven (Heb. 2:17).

   c. Christ is able to sympathize with our weaknesses. He is a priest who identifies with and understands the mental and physical frailities of mankind, having been a man Himself (Heb. 4:15-16).

   d. Christ, therefore, is a priest who represents men with empathy before the Father.

   e. He is a perfect priest because He has taken sin upon Himself and yet, at the same time, is unblemished and sinless. He is the only one in the universe able to truly represent the human situation (Heb. 7:26).

3. We receive God's full mercy today because Christ, who is God, fully identified and empathized with our situation.

B. Christ Experienced the Full Effect of Man's Sin

1. He experienced the poverty of a lowly birth. There was nothing romantic about being born among the stench of cattle (Lk. 2:7).

LESSON TWO · JESUS CHRIST: GOD'S MERCY IN ACTION

IV. HOW DID CHRIST ACCOMPLISH HIS PURPOSE?

Matthew 8:20
Jesus replied, "Foxes have holes and birds of the air have nests, but the Son of Man has no place to lay his head."

Matthew 26:38-39
Then he said to them, "My soul is overwhelmed with sorrow to the point of death. Stay here and keep watch with me." [39]Going a little farther, he fell with his face to the ground and prayed, "My Father, if it is possible, may this cup be taken from me. Yet not as I will, but as you will."

Luke 19:41-44
As he approached Jerusalem and saw the city, he wept over it. [42]and said, "If you, even you, had only known on this day what would bring you peace—but now it is hidden from your eyes. [43]The days will come upon you when your enemies will build an embankment against you and encircle you and hem you in on every side. [44]They will dash you to the ground, you and the children within your walls. They will not leave one stone on another, because you did not recognize the time of God's coming to you."

John 19:1-2
Then Pilate took Jesus and had him flogged. [2]The soldiers twisted together a crown of thorns and put it on his head. They clothed him in a purple robe.

Isaiah 52:14
Just as there were many who were appalled at him—his appearance was so disfigured beyond that of any man and his form marred beyond human likeness.

Mark 15:34
And at the ninth hour Jesus cried out in a loud voice, "*Eloi, Eloi, lama sabachthani?*"—which means, "My God, my God, why have you forsaken me?"

2 Corinthians 5:21
God made him who had no sin to be sin for us, so that in him we might become the righteousness of God.

Hebrews 9:12-14
He did not enter by means of the blood of goats and calves; but he entered the Most Holy Place once for all by his own blood, having obtained eternal redemption. [13]The blood of goats and bulls and the ashes of a heifer sprinkled on those who are ceremonially unclean sanctify them so that they are outwardly clean. [14]How much more, then, will the blood of Christ, who through the eternal Spirit offered himself unblemished to God, cleanse our consciences from acts that lead to death, so that we may serve the living God!

2. He experienced poverty in his childhood. Joseph and Mary were peasants living on the lower end of the social scale.

3. He experienced poverty in His life-style. Christ said the foxes have a place to go, but the Son of man has no place to lay His head (Mt. 8:20).

4. He experienced the bankruptcy of the human condition brought on by sin. He felt the full effect of man's struggle in every aspect of His existence:

   a. *Spiritual Struggle*   He struggled in the Garden of Gethsemane with the implications of completely fulfilling the Father's will for His life (Mt. 26:38-39, 42, 44).

   b. *Mental Struggle*   Jesus wept. He knew what it was to feel great mental anguish as He wept over the needs of lost people (Lk. 19:41-44).

   c. *Physical Agony*   Jesus was beaten, scourged, and crucified for all of humanity. Isaiah prophesied this terrible mutilation of Jesus Christ (Jn. 19:1-2; Isa. 52:14, 53:4-5).

5. He experienced the full weight of human sin and guilt even to the point of losing touch with the Father. Jesus tasted death for every man (Mk. 15:34; Heb. 2:9).

C. Christ Became the Perfect Sacrifice for Man

1. Christ perfectly atoned for sin. Man's past, present, and future sins were put upon Jesus Christ and judged by God. Only Christ's unblemished death could appease God's judgment on man's sin. The fact that He never yielded to sin made Him the perfect, unblemished sacrifice (2 Cor. 5:21).

2. Throughout the Old Testament, God required sacrifices for sin. The Old Testament sacrifice of animals only postponed God's judgment. Christ, however, was the true and fully adequate sacrifice that satisfied God's wrath against sin forever (Heb. 9:12-14).

LESSON TWO · JESUS CHRIST: GOD'S MERCY IN ACTION

IV. HOW DID CHRIST ACCOMPLISH HIS PURPOSE?

Exodus 12:5
The animals you choose must be year-old males without defect, and you may take them from the sheep or the goats.

John 1:29
The next day John saw Jesus coming toward him and said, "Look, the Lamb of God, who takes away the sin of the world!"

Isaiah 53:7
He was oppressed and afflicted, yet he did not open his mouth; he was led like a lamb to the slaughter, and as a sheep before her shearers is silent, so he did not open his mouth.

Exodus 12:46
"It must be eaten inside one house; take none of the meat outside the house. Do not break any of the bones. 47The whole community of Israel must celebrate it."

Leviticus 16:5
From the Israelite community he is to take two male goats for a sin offering and a ram for a burnt offering.

Leviticus 16:11-14
"Aaron shall bring the bull for his own sin offering to make atonement for himself and his household, and he is to slaughter the bull for his own sin offering. 12He is to take a censer full of burning coals from the altar before the LORD and two handfuls of finely ground fragrant incense and take them behind the curtain. 13He is to put the incense on the fire before the LORD, and the smoke of the incense will conceal the atonement cover above the Testimony, so that he will not die. 14He is to take some of the bull's blood and with his finger sprinkle it on the front of the atonement cover; then he shall sprinkle some of it with his finger seven times before the atonement cover.

Leviticus 16:8
He is to cast lots for the two goats—one lot for the LORD and the other for the scapegoat.

3. The Old Testament symbolism of sacrifice was fully realized in Jesus Christ.

   a. *Exodus 12:5* The Passover regulations required that a Lamb without blemish or defect be slaughtered. The blood was to be put over the door of every household as a protective covering. Christ was the sinless, unblemished Lamb of God whose shed blood protects the sinner from God's wrath (Jn. 1:29).

   b. *Isaiah 53:7* Isaiah prophesied of Christ being led like a lamb to the slaughter. He did not defend Himself at His trial even though the accusations were false (Mt. 27:11-14).

   c. *Exodus 12:46* The bones of the Passover Lamb were not to be broken. Since Christ bled to death on the cross, it was not necessary to break his legs and thus hasten death by suffocation. This was done, however, in the case of the two thieves so that the bodies could be removed before the Sabbath began (Jn. 19:32-36).

D. Christ Carried Away Man's Sin Forever

1. In the Old Testament, three animals were used in the sacrifice offered every year for Israel's sin (Lev. 16:5):

   a. Two male goats

   b. One male ram

2. Aaron, the high priest, was to make atonement for himself and his house first by offering the male ram as a sacrifice. This would cover him as one who was ceremonially cleansed and thus fit as a priest to offer an additional sacrifice for people (Lev. 16:11-14).

3. Aaron then cast lots over the heads of the two unblemished male goats. The goat on which the lot fell was to be slain and offered as a blood sacrifice for the sins of the people (Lev. 16:8).

Pathway of Discipleship

LESSON TWO · JESUS CHRIST: GOD'S MERCY IN ACTION

IV. HOW DID CHRIST ACCOMPLISH HIS PURPOSE?

Leviticus 16:10, 20-22
But the goat chosen by lot as the scapegoat shall be presented alive before the LORD to be used for making atonement by sending it into the desert as a scapegoat.

"When Aaron has finished making atonement for the Most Holy Place, the Tent of Meeting and the altar, he shall bring forward the live goat. 21He is to lay both hands on the head of the live goat and confess over it all the wickedness and rebellion of the Israelites—all their sins—and put them on the goat's head. He shall send the goat away into the desert in the care of a man appointed for the task. 22The goat will carry on itself all their sins to a solitary place; and the man shall release it in the desert."

Romans 4:25
He was delivered over to death for our sins and was raised to life for our justification.

Ephesians 2:4-5
But because of his great love for us, God, who is rich in mercy, 5made us alive with Christ even when we were dead in transgressions—it is by grace you have been saved.

Titus 3:5
He saved us, not because of righteous things we had done, but because of his mercy. He saved us through the washing of rebirth and renewal by the Holy Spirit.

Romans 12:2
Do not conform any longer to the pattern of this world, but be transformed by the renewing of your mind. Then you will be able to test and approve what God's will is—his good, pleasing and perfect will.

Colossians 1:27
To them God has chosen to make known among the Gentiles the glorious riches of this mystery, which is Christ in you, the hope of glory.

4. The second goat was to become known as the scapegoat. After offering the first goat to God, Aaron was to confess the sins of the people and literally lay his hands on the goat, symbolically putting all the sins of the people on the live goat (Lev. 16:10, 20-22).

5. The goat was then led into the wilderness to die with all the sins of the people upon it.

6. Tradition has it that the scapegoat was actually pushed over a cliff to assure its death.

7. This Old Testament ceremony was a symbol of the perfect scapegoat who was to come, Jesus Christ.

8. Christ took every sin of man upon Himself and allowed Himself to die bearing the full weight of all sin. In so doing, He eliminated man's sin and carried it away forever.

E. Christ Rose from the Dead

1. His resurrection ultimately accomplished God's will to fully redeem and restore mankind. It signified that God had accepted Christ's death for our sins and, therefore, we could be justified or cleared of all guilt (Ro. 4:25).

2. At conversion, God joins with man's spirit. Man is regenerated with divine life. The Holy Spirit enters man and begins to quicken him from within (Eph. 2:4-5).

3. The Holy Spirit, God's divine life, immediately begins the restorative work of God's kingdom. He brings renewal to the total situation (Tit. 3:5).

4. The chief purpose of this divine life is to renew the Christian's thinking. It is to sanctify and continually change the mind-soul area of man into a reflection of Christ's image within (Ro. 12:2). Colossians chapters 1, 2 and 3 bear this out.

Chapter One Christ's life lives within (Col. 1:27).

LESSON TWO · JESUS CHRIST: GOD'S MERCY IN ACTION

IV. HOW DID CHRIST ACCOMPLISH HIS PURPOSE?

Colossians 2:6-7
So then, just as you received Christ Jesus as Lord, continue to live in him, [7]rooted and built up in him, strengthened in the faith as you were taught, and overflowing with thankfulness.

Colossians 3:2, 8-10
Set your minds on things above, not on earthly things.

But now you must rid yourselves of all such things as these: anger, rage, malice, slander, and filthy language from your lips. [9]Do not lie to each other, since you have taken off your old self with its practices [10]and have put on the new self, which is being renewed in knowledge in the image of its Creator.

Acts 1:8
"But you will receive power when the Holy Spirit comes on you; and you will be my witnesses in Jerusalem, and in all Judea and Samaria, and to the ends of the earth."

Ephesians 1:13-14
And you also were included in Christ when you heard the word of truth, the gospel of your salvation. Having believed, you were marked in him with a seal, the promised Holy Spirit, [14]who is a deposit guaranteeing our inheritance until the redemption of those who are God's possessions—to the praise of his glory.

James 5:14-15
Is any one of you sick? He should call the elders of the church to pray over him and anoint him with oil in the name of the Lord. [15]And the prayer offered in faith will make the sick person well; the Lord will raise him up. If he has sinned, he will be forgiven.

Mark 11:22-24
"Have faith in God," Jesus answered. [23]"I tell you the truth, if anyone says to this mountain, 'Go, throw yourself into the sea,' and does not doubt in his heart but believes that what he says will happen, it will be done for him. [24]Therefore I tell you, whatever you ask for in prayer, believe that you have received it, and it will be yours."

Chapter Two The Christian is to yield continually to the changing power of Christ's life within (Col. 2:6-7).

Chapter Three The power of this life brings a change of mind as well as a change in behavior (Col. 3:2, 8-10).

5. The second purpose of this divine life within is to use the individual as a channel of life to others:

In the last day, that great day of the feast, Jesus stood and cried, saying, If any man thirst, let him come unto me, and drink. He that believeth on me, as the scripture hath said, out of his belly shall flow rivers of living water. But this spake he of the Spirit, which they that believe on him should receive.

(Jn. 7:37-39, KJV)

This flow of living water comes with the Holy Spirit's full inner release and empowering. (Acts 1:8).

6. The third purpose of the divine life is to allow man, through faith, to experience a portion of the complete restoration which is to come. We have been given the Holy Spirit as a down payment on our eternal inheritance (Eph. 1:13-14).

Example: We experience a taste of physical renewal in the divine healing of our bodies through prayer (Jas. 5:14-15).

7. This inner life of Christ through faith gives a person the potential of experiencing victory over every circumstance of life (Mk. 11:22-24).

8. In saying the above we must realize the fact of God's sovereignty and discipline. God's will is to mold us, to bring forth the qualities of the kingdom in us. It is as the believer seeks the fruits of His kingdom that is, as he lets the Father mold and discipline and bring forth the qualities of Jesus Christ, that he begins to experience the blessings of God's kingdom as well.

F. Conclusion

We can see in all of the ways that Christ went about accomplishing His purpose, He was indeed the embodiment of God's mercy taking action in our world.

1. He identified with our condition.

2. He experienced the full effects of our sin.

3. He was the perfect sacrifice on our behalf.

4. He carried away our sins forever.

5. He was resurrected for our justification.

V. SUMMATION

1. Christ's coming represents the ultimate expression of God's mercy toward a sinful and hurting world.

2. Jesus Christ was God's love in action. He was the Word. He was God. He came as the Creator, the source of all true life and light. He was the Word of God in human flesh.

3. Christ came in order to bring God's re-creative life to man. He came to begin a work of restoration. He came as well to reveal God's character and His ways to mankind.

4. When He came, Christ fully identified with our human condition. He personally experienced the full effects of our guilt, dying as the perfect sacrifice which carried away our sins forever. Then He rose from the dead so that we could fully and permanently experience divine life.

103

home study guide

LESSON TWO · DAY ONE

SECTIONS I · II

1. Why are the cross, the empty tomb, and the events of the Day of Pentecost essential to God's work of restoration among fallen mankind?

_____

_____

_____

_____

_____

2. Study John 5:12-24 and discuss all that it implies about who Jesus Christ really was?

_____

_____

_____

_____

_____

_____

_____

_____

_____

_____

3. In a study of God's mercy and what it means to become merciful, why is it important that we understand who Jesus Christ was?

_____

_____

_____

_____

4. In what area of our lives has God chosen to begin His work of total healing and restoration—physical, social, mental, or spiritual? Give scripture references for your answer.

_____

_____

_____

_____

_____

_____

home study guide

LESSON TWO · DAY TWO

SECTION III

1. a. What were Christ's two basic purposes in coming to this world? Jn. 10:10, 14:8-10

_____

_____

_____

_____

_____

_____

   b. Suggest some scriptures that express or illustrate these two purposes.

_____

_____

_____

_____

_____

_____

_____

2. Explain the significance of John 1:4 in the light of Ephesians 2:1-3, 5:8.

_____

_____

_____

_____

_____

3. a. How will the condition of totally restored man differ from Adam's condition before the Fall Ro. 8:16-17

_____

_____

_____

_____

   b. How will it be the same?

_____

_____

_____

_____

home study guide

LESSON TWO · DAY THREE

SECTION IV

1. How did Christ identify with the human condition? Heb. 2:14

_____

_____

_____

2. Give two reasons why it was essential that Christ become a genuine human being? Gal. 4:4-5; Heb. 2:17, 10:4

   a. _____

_____

_____

_____

_____

   b. _____

_____

_____

_____

_____

3. a. Using Isaiah 53:4-12 as a basis, describe how Christ became the perfect sacrifice for man.

_____

_____

_____

_____

_____

_____

_____

_____

   b. In what ways does the passage above relate Christ's death to the Father's plan of restoration?

_____

_____

_____

_____

home study guide

LESSON TWO · DAY FOUR

SECTION IV

1. What do Christ's resurrection and His ascension to sit at the Father's right hand say to us about the all-sufficient and complete nature of His sacrifice for our sin? Heb. 10:1-14.

_____

_____

_____

_____

_____

_____

_____

2. Briefly describe the three purposes for which God's life is placed in the believer at conversion in the form of the indwelling Holy Spirit.

(1) _____

_____

_____

_____

(2) _____

_____

_____

_____

(3) _____

_____

_____

_____

3. Explain some of the things involved in yielding to the power of the indwelling Holy Spirit. Ro. 8:2-8

_____

_____

_____

_____

_____

_____

_____

_____

PATHWAY of Discipleship

home study guide

LESSON TWO · DAY FIVE

SECTION IV

1. God wants us to experience the benefits of His kingdom, but beyond that, what does He desire to do with us?

   _____
   _____
   _____
   _____

2. If we are to know the blessings of the kingdom, what will we have to submit ourselves to?

   _____
   _____
   _____
   _____

3. What does Christ's complete and costly identification with the situation of fallen humanity say to you about the personal cost of becoming God's mercy to your community?

   _____
   _____
   _____
   _____
   _____

4. Suggest some practical ways that you could begin to identify with the deep needs of non-Christians in your community.

   _____
   _____
   _____
   _____
   _____
   _____
   _____
   _____
   _____
   _____
   _____
   _____

LESSON THREE · THE WORLD-WIDE STRATEGY OF JESUS CHRIST

OUTLINE

Lesson Three Update

Lesson Three Synopsis

I. **HE BEGAN WITH HIMSELF**
   A. Jesus Proclaimed
   B. Jesus Demonstrated

II. **HE CHOSE TWELVE MEN**
   A. A Startling Fact
   B. Eight Principles

III. **HE COMMISSIONED HIS CHURCH**
   A. To Multiply and to Continue His Earthly Ministry
   B. To Continue to Proclaim the Kingdom
   C. To Continue to Demonstrate the Kingdom

IV. **HE EMPOWERED HIS CHURCH**
   A. On the Day of Pentecost
   B. He Continues to Empower His Church

V. **SUMMATION**

Home Study Guide

LESSON THREE - THE WORLD-WIDE STRATEGY OF JESUS CHRIST

LESSON THREE UPDATE

Lesson One   Jesus Christ was the full revelation of God's mercy to the world. Those who are merciful respond to the needs of the world in the same way that Jesus did. Like the Good Samaritan, the merciful take compassionate action on behalf of the total needs of people.

Lesson Two   Jesus Christ was God's mercy in action in our world. Through His life, death, and resurrection, God began a work of restoration in His fallen creation. God the Son who was the Creator, the Light, the Word, and the Life, came to bring God's re-creative life to mankind. He also came to reveal God's character and ways to mankind. He accomplished His life-giving and revelatory purposes by fully identifying with men. He became a man and gave Himself as the perfect sacrifice for the sins of men. After He paid the penalty of sin and destroyed its power, He rose from the dead so that He could permanently impart God's life to all who would receive it through faith.

LESSON THREE · THE WORLD-WIDE STRATEGY OF JESUS CHRIST

LESSON THREE SYNOPSIS

What was the strategy of Jesus Christ? How would all men hear the message He brought and how would those who received it be motivated and trained to carry to others this message of eternal life?

Christ began the work of bringing life to the world with Himself. For three years He proclaimed and demonstrated the kingdom of God in accordance with His prophetic mandate given in Luke 4:18-19.

The next step in Christ's strategy was to chose twelve men to intensively train. He literally poured His life into these men for three years to prepare them to take the message to the multitudes.

Just before returning to heaven, Christ commissioned His fledgling Church to grow and multiply while continuing His ministry of proclaiming and demonstrating the kingdom.

Again after His ascension, the final stage of His strategy was completed with the sending of the Holy Spirit to empower and fully equip the Church to go forth with authority and begin to inaugurate the kingdom of God among men.

Pathway of Discipleship

I. HE BEGAN WITH HIMSELF

I. HE BEGAN WITH HIMSELF

Christ's entire earthly ministry was one of proclamation and demonstration. He proclaimed and demonstrated the Good News of total redemption through His death and resurrection to come. He was here to bring forth the kingdom.

A. Jesus Proclaimed

1. In Luke 4:18-19, He announced His message and purpose for coming:

   a. "The Spirit of the Lord is on me, because he has anointed me to preach good news to the poor. He has sent me to proclaim freedom for the prisoners and recovery of sight for the blind, to release the oppressed, to proclaim the year of the Lord's favor."

      This is what God had set Him aside and chosen Him to do. This was Christ's special anointing.

   b. Notice the wholistic approach of Christ's message. He came to minister to man's total needs:

      (1) Good news for those who are spiritually or physically impoverished.

      (2) Freedom for prisoners, those who are bound by habits and the power of Satan.

      (3) Recovery of sight for those spiritually and physically blind.

      (4) Release for those who are oppressed by Satan and the evil restraints of ungodly men.

   c. Christ also came to proclaim the year of the Lord's favor. This was the dawning of the era of salvation. Up until this time, men felt hopeless. With the Old Testament sacrificial system, there was only a temporary reprieve of God's judgment for another year, not eternal salvation. It could not be obtained. In proclaiming the year of the Lord's

Romans 8:16-23
The Spirit himself testifies with our spirit that we are God's children. [17] Now if we are children, then we are heirs—heirs of God and co-heirs with Christ, if indeed we share in his sufferings in order that we may also share in his glory.

[18] I consider that our present sufferings are not worth comparing with the glory that will be revealed in us. [19] The creation waits in eager expectation for the sons of God to be revealed. [20] For the creation was subjected to frustration, not by its own choice, but by the will of the one who subjected it, in hope [21] that the creation itself will be liberated from its bondage to decay and brought into the glorious freedom of the children of God.

LESSON THREE · THE WORLD-WIDE STRATEGY OF JESUS CHRIST

II. HE CHOSE TWELVE MEN

²²We know that the whole creation has been groaning as in the pains of childbirth right up to the present time. ²³Not only so, but we ourselves, who have the firstfruits of the Spirit, groan inwardly as we wait eagerly for our adoption as sons, the redemption of our bodies.

John 14:7-11
"If you really knew me, you would know my Father as well. From now on, you do know him and have seen him." ⁸Philip said, "Lord, show us the Father and that will be enough for us."
⁹Jesus answered: "Don't you know me, Philip, even after I have been among you such a long time? Anyone who has seen me has seen the Father. How can you say, 'Show us the Father'? ¹⁰Don't you believe that I am in the Father, and that the Father is in me? The words I say to you are not just my own. Rather, it is the Father, living in me, who is doing his work. ¹¹Believe me when I say that I am in the Father and the Father is in me; or at least believe on the evidence of the miracles themselves.

Luke 3:21-22
When all the people were being baptized, Jesus was baptized too. And as he was praying heaven was opened ²²and the Holy Spirit descended on him in bodily form like a dove. And a voice came from heaven: "You are my Son, whom I love; with you I am well pleased."

Luke 4:16-19
He went to Nazareth, where he had been brought up, and on the Sabbath day he went into the synagogue, as was his custom. And he stood up to read. ¹⁷The scroll of the prophet Isaiah was handed to him. Unrolling it, he found the place where it is written:
¹⁸"The Spirit of the Lord is on me,
  because he has anointed me
  to preach good news to the poor.
He has sent me to proclaim freedom
    for the prisoners
  and recovery of sight for the blind,
  to release the oppressed,
¹⁹ to proclaim the year of the Lord's favor."

Luke 4:33-35
In the synagogue there was a man possessed by a demon, an evil spirit. He cried out at the top of his voice, ³⁴"Ha! What do you want with us, Jesus of Nazareth? Have you come to destroy us? I know who you are—the Holy One of God!"
³⁵"Be quiet!" Jesus said sternly. "Come out of him!" Then the demon threw the man down before them all and came out without injuring him.

favor, Jesus was saying, this is the beginning of a new kingdom. Men may come and know God's gift of eternal life here and now. They can taste of the firstfruits of a tremendous eternal inheritance God is preparing for them in the age to come (Ro. 8:16-23).

B. Jesus Demonstrated

1. With every miracle Jesus performed He was demonstrating the Father's mercy and His ultimate will for His fallen creation (Jn. 14:7-11).

2. In Luke's narrative we see, in a vivid sequence, the development of Jesus Christ's ministry:

   a. Luke 3:21-22   At His baptism Jesus is publicly declared to be chosen and anointed by God.

   b. Luke 4:1-13   He is tested and made ready for ministry.

   c. Luke 4:16-19   He begins to proclaim the gospel.

   d. Luke 4:33-35   He begins to demonstrate the gospel.

3. There could never be any question of Jesus proclaiming, but not practicing. As He preached the Good News of God's mercy, He also demonstrated the mercy of God by healing sick bodies, feeding hungry multitudes, and taking action against those who oppressed others.

II. HE CHOSE TWELVE MEN

A. A Startling Fact

1. Perhaps the most startling and obvious fact concerning the strategy of Jesus Christ in winning the world was that He concentrated most of His three or four short years of public ministry on twelve people. During those years He taught and demonstrated to them everything they needed to know about His kingdom.

LESSON THREE · THE WORLD-WIDE STRATEGY
OF JESUS CHRIST

II. HE CHOSE TWELVE MEN

2. Robert E. Coleman in *The Master Plan of Evangelism,* an excellent analysis of Jesus' use of the small group as a teaching method, comments:

> One cannot transform a world except as individuals in the world are transformed, and individuals cannot be changed except as they are molded in the hands of the Master. The necessity is apparent not only to select a few laymen, but to keep the group small enough to be able to work effectively with them.[1]

3. Concerning the fact that Jesus gave preference to the Twelve, Coleman writes:

> All of this certainly impresses us with the deliberate way that Jesus proportioned His life to those He wanted to train. It also graphically illustrates a fundamental principle of teaching: that other things being equal, the more concentrated the size of the group being taught, the greater the opportunity for effective instruction.[2]

4. In applying this principle from the ministry of Jesus to our own day, Professor Coleman notes:

> Surely if the pattern of Jesus at this point means anything at all it teaches that the first duty of a pastor as well as the first concern of an evangelist is to see to it that a foundation is laid in the beginning upon which can be built an effective and continuing evangelistic ministry to the multitudes. This will require more concentration of time and talents upon fewer men in the church while not neglecting the passion for the world. It will mean raising up trained leadership 'for the work of ministering' with the pastor (Ephesians 4:12). A few people so dedicated in time will shake the world for God. Victory is never won by the multitudes.[3]

B. Eight Principles

Professor Coleman gives eight principles Jesus used in discipling the Twelve:

1. *Selection*   He specifically chose twelve men.

2. *Association*   He lived with them and they learned His ways.

---

[1] Robert E. Coleman, *The Master Plan of Evangelism*, (Fleming H. Revell, 1975), p. 24.
[2] Coleman, pp. 26-27
[3] Coleman, pp. 33-34

103

Pathway of Discipleship

LESSON THREE · THE WORLD-WIDE STRATEGY OF JESUS CHRIST

III. HE COMMISSIONED HIS CHURCH

---

3. *Concentration*   He concentrated His efforts upon them.

4. *Impartation*   He imparted His life and purpose to them. He expected them to carry on His work.

5. *Demonstration*   He demonstrated to them what He came to do and what He expected them to do.

6. *Delegation*   He delegated various tasks to them.

7. *Supervision*   He supervised them as they carried out the tasks He delegated to them.

8. *Reproduction*   He reproduced Himself in them. All that He was He tried to impart to these twelve men.

After three years of training before His death, and forty days of instruction after His resurrection, Jesus turned the disciples loose. In John 20:21 He told the disciples that He was sending them into the world to do the same things that the Father had sent Him into the world to do. He was sending them to proclaim and demonstrate the gospel just as He had done in accordance with Luke 4:18-19.

III. HE COMMISSIONED HIS CHURCH

A. To Multiply and to Continue His Earthly Ministry

1. The Twelve had been trained to lay the foundations for an earthly body of people that would extend the ministry of Jesus Christ all over the world (Eph. 2:19-20).

2. Christ was the cornerstone perfectly supporting the entire structure. Without Him it would fold. The Twelve were to begin building the foundation of the Church upon Christ. They had learned His words and ways for three years.

John 20:21
Again Jesus said, "Peace be with you! As the Father has sent me, I am sending you."

Ephesians 2:19-20
Consequently, you are no longer foreigners and aliens, but fellow citizens with God's people and members of God's household, ²⁰built on the foundation of the apostles and prophets, with Christ Jesus himself as the chief cornerstone.

LESSON THREE · THE WORLD-WIDE STRATEGY OF JESUS CHRIST

III. HE COMMISSIONED HIS CHURCH

Matthew 28:19-20
"Therefore go and make disciples of all nations, baptizing them in the name of the Father and of the Son and of the Holy Spirit, [20] and teaching them to obey everything I have commanded you. And surely I will be with you always, to the very end of the age."

Colossians 1:13
For he has rescued us from the dominion of darkness and brought us into the kingdom of the Son he loves.

Matthew 6:33
But seek first his kingdom and his righteousness, and all these things will be given to you as well.

Ephesians 6:15
And with your feet fitted with the readiness that comes from the gospel of peace.

Mark 10:1
Jesus then left that place and went into the region of Judea and across the Jordan. Again crowds of people came to him, and as was his custom, he taught them.

Acts 2:41
Those who accepted his message were baptized, and about three thousand were added to their number that day.

Acts 8:5-6
Philip went down to a city in Samaria and proclaimed the Christ there. [6]When the crowds heard Philip and saw the miraculous signs he did, they all paid close attention to what he said.

3. The Twelve were to repeat the process of discipleship in other men's lives as Christ had done with them. They were to apply the principle of multiplication (Mt. 28:19-20).

B. To Continue to Proclaim the Kingdom

1. The church is to proclaim this message of total redemption. The church is to challenge men to believe in Jesus Christ; to step from the kingdom of this world (darkness) into the kingdom of God's dear Son (Col. 1:13).

2. The church is to proclaim that now is the acceptable year of the Lord (Lk. 4:18-19). Now men can begin to receive the provisions of God's kingdom. As the kingdom becomes their life's pursuit, all of God's provisions within that kingdom become theirs (Mt. 6:33).

3. Every believer must be trained to know how to lead a person to Jesus Christ. Every believer must be ready when the right moment comes to clearly articulate the Good News (Eph. 6:15).

4. In addition to this, it is God's will to proclaim the message to the multitudes "through the foolishness of preaching" (1 Cor. 1:21, KJV). Mass evangelism has always been a method God uses to reach the multitudes—in the life of Jesus (Mk. 5:21, 10:1) and in the life of the early church (Acts 2:41, 8:5-6).

C. To Continue to Demonstrate the Kingdom

1. The work of God's Spirit in our lives begins to help us view the world as God does. The worldly philosophy within us may cause us to write off certain people because they are lazy. They do not try to help themselves and so forth. The godly man, however, looks with pity and sympathy upon all men. God's love within the believer helps him not to judge others. It is a never-ending love reaching out to pick up, restore, heal, and save every person. Each disciple has one goal: to raise the physical, mental, and spiritual standards of each individual's life, and to see

III. HE COMMISSIONED HIS CHURCH

John 15:1-8
"I am the true vine and my Father is the gardener. ²He cuts off every branch in me that bears no fruit, while every branch that does bear fruit he trims clean so that it will be even more fruitful. ³You are already clean because of the word I have spoken to you. ⁴Remain in me, and I will remain in you. No branch can bear fruit by itself; it must remain in the vine. Neither can you bear fruit unless you remain in me.
⁵"I am the vine; you are the branches. If a man remains in me and I in him, he will bear much fruit; apart from me you can do nothing. ⁶If anyone does not remain in me, he is like a branch that is thrown away and withers; such branches are picked up, thrown into the fire and burned. ⁷If you remain in me and my words remain in you, ask whatever you wish, and it will be given you. ⁸This is to my Father's glory, that you bear much fruit, showing yourselves to be my disciples.

him completely transformed through the power of God's Spirit.

2. As has been stated, this compassion can only be ours through the work of God's Spirit. Like all the other principles of God's kingdom, being merciful does not come naturally. It is most often opposite to how the world views the same person or problem. It can only be produced in our lives as we allow God to work in us.

3. In demonstrating the will of God for fallen mankind, individuals and the local church must work in conjunction with the Lord's leading. Only through prayer and waiting on God (drawing constantly on the strength of the vine, Jn. 15:1-8) can we meet the needs of wounded humanity. Jesus said, "If you abide in me (wait upon me), and my words abide in you (you submit to my Word), ask whatever you will, and it shall be done for you" (v. 7, RSV, paraphrases added).

4. A body of believers who live in vital union with Christ can go forth as the early disciples did, with complete authority over the enemy, who, although he has been totally defeated, still fights to keep man wallowing in his hopeless condition. In the authority of Christ's name, the Church is to soothe and heal every wound, to lift up the fallen, and to bring hope to every aspect of people's lives.

5. Whether we minister on the human or supernatural plane, the enemy will fight and frustrate our efforts unless we live in the place of prayer and vital union with Christ. This walk of fellowship with Christ is the thing that precipitates our desire to help a needy world and empowers us to get the job done effectively. Knowing the necessity of this attitude of poverty of spirit, of living in constant vital union with Christ through prayer, the Church goes forth to minister to man's needs on every level.

6. God calls His Church to have compassion on every aspect of man's marred being. The Church must become involved in:

LESSON THREE · THE WORLD-WIDE STRATEGY OF JESUS CHRIST

IV. HE EMPOWERED HIS CHURCH

Mark 16:17-19
And these signs will accompany those who believe: In my name they will drive out demons; they will speak in new tongues; ¹⁸they will pick up snakes with their hands; and when they drink deadly poison, it will not hurt them at all; they will place their hands on sick people, and they will get well."

¹⁹After the Lord Jesus had spoken to them, he was taken up into heaven and he sat at the right hand of God.

1 Corinthians 12:8-10
To one there is given through the Spirit the message of wisdom, to another the message of knowledge by means of the same Spirit, ⁹to another faith by the same Spirit, to another gifts of healing by that one Spirit, ¹⁰to another miraculous powers, to another prophecy, to another the ability to distinguish between spirits, to another the ability to speak in different kinds of tongues, and to still another the interpretation of tongues.

Luke 24:49
"I am going to send you what my Father has promised; but stay in the city until you have been clothed with power from on high."

Acts 1:5, 8
For John baptized with water, but in a few days you will be baptized with the Holy Spirit.

⁸"But you will receive power when the Holy Spirit comes on you; and you will be my witnesses in Jerusalem, and in all Judea and Samaria, and to the ends of the earth."

Acts 2:1-4
When the day of Pentecost came, they were all together in one place. ²Suddenly a sound like the blowing of a violent wind came from heaven and filled the whole house where they were sitting. ³They saw what seemed to be tongues of fire that separated and came to rest on each of them. ⁴All of them were filled with the Holy Spirit and began to speak in other tongues as the Spirit enabled them.

a. Evangelism with signs following (Mk. 16:17-19).

b. Combatting the hunger problem around the world.

c. Establishing hospitals and schools.

d. Providing counseling services.

e. Outreaches to help the fallen: rehabilitation programs, inner-city missions, clothing programs, and so forth.

This is the mercy of God in action.

7. In the midst of ministry to man's total need, God has given to the Church nine supernatural manifestations of the Holy Spirit (1 Cor. 12:8-10). These manifestations allow the supernatural ministry of Christ to continue through His body, the Church (Jn. 14:16-20).

IV. HE EMPOWERED HIS CHURCH

A. On the Day of Pentecost

1. Just before leaving the earth, Jesus gave the disciples a command and a promise:

   a. The command was to wait in the city of Jerusalem until they were clothed with God's power (Lu. 24:49).

   b. The promise was that He would soon fill them with the Holy Spirit and thus empower them to be His witnesses (Acts 1:5, 8).

2. It is important to note that although Christ had already commissioned the apostles to make disciples of all the nations, He told them not to begin to proclaim the gospel until they had received His divine empowering (Mt. 28:19-20).

3. The disciples waited in Jerusalem until the Day of Pentecost when they were empowered with the Holy Spirit (Acts 2:1-4).

103

V. SUMMATION

John 16:7
But I tell you the truth: It is for your good that I am going away. Unless I go away, the Counselor will not come to you; but if I go, I will send him to you.

Acts 4:31
After they prayed, the place where they were meeting was shaken. And they were all filled with the Holy Spirit and spoke the word of God boldly.

Acts 10:44-46
While Peter was still speaking these words, the Holy Spirit came on all who heard the message. [45] The circumcised believers who had come with Peter were astonished that the gift of the Holy Spirit had been poured out even on the Gentiles. [46] For they heard them speaking in tongues and praising God.

John 7:37-38
On the last and greatest day of the Feast, Jesus stood and said in a loud voice, "If a man is thirsty, let him come to me and drink. [38] Whoever believes in me, as the Scripture has said, streams of living water will flow from within him."

4. The immediate result was that Peter (the very one who had so cowardly denied Christ) preached a sermon which brought 3,000 people into the Church (Acts chapter 2).

5. The sending of the Spirit upon the Church was essential to Christ's world-wide strategy. By Himself, He could never have reached the whole world with the gospel. This is why He told the disciples that it was to their advantage that He return to the Father so that the Spirit would be sent (Jn. 16:7). With the Holy Spirit coming to indwell every believer, a vast army could be raised up of people filled with God's life and power who could be sent out to proclaim and demonstrate the gospel all over the globe.

B. He Continues to Empower His Church

1. We read throughout the rest of the book of Acts that believers were empowered to proclaim and demonstrate the gospel (Acts 4:31, 10:44-46, 19:6).

2. Today He continues to baptize believers with the Holy Spirit, empowering them to both proclaim and demonstrate the gospel as He did. As we minister to people in need, out of our innermost being flow rivers of living water (Jn. 7:37-38). This living water is the resurrection power of Jesus Christ coming forth from the lives of Spirit-filled individuals to heal and set free, bringing:

a. Good news to the poor.

b. Freedom for the prisoners.

c. Recovery of sight to the blind.

d. Release to the oppressed.

e. The proclamation of the year of the Lord's favor.

V. SUMMATION

1. Jesus Christ inaugurated the work of God's mercy on earth by proclaiming and demonstrating the

56

V. SUMMATION

coming of the kingdom of God among men. This was in accordance with the prophecy of Isaiah 61:1-2 as quoted in Luke 4:18-19.

2. The next step in Christ's strategy was to select and intensively train twelve men who would in turn be able to win and train others.

3. Christ then gave His Church the charge to multiply and continue His earthly ministry of proclaiming and demonstrating the kingdom.

4. Finally, Jesus empowered the Church on the Day of Pentecost with the Holy Spirit and continues to empower her today to complete the task of bringing God's mercy to our world in word and deed.

home study guide

LESSON THREE · DAY ONE

SECTION I

1. Why is Luke 4:18-19 crucial to our understanding of the ministry of Jesus Christ?

_____

_____

_____

_____

2. Read Romans 8:16-25 and then describe the tension that exists between our experience of salvation now and in eternity.

_____

_____

_____

_____

_____

_____

3. How do Christ's miracles relate to His purpose in coming to earth?

_____

_____

_____

_____

4. Study John 9:1-7 and explain how Christ's actions and His teaching on this occasion are related to God's mercy for fallen man.

_____

_____

_____

_____

_____

home study guide

LESSON THREE · DAY TWO

SECTION II

1. Reread the quotations from Robert Coleman's book found in the notes.
   a. Why did Jesus give so much of His time to training only twelve men?

   _____

   _____

   _____

   _____

   b. What does Christ's strategy in reaching the world say to you about the importance of the small group in the local church?

   _____

   _____

   _____

   _____

   _____

   c. What does His strategy say to you about how your pastor should spend most of his time?

   _____

   _____

   _____

   _____

   _____

   _____

2. a. Describe the relationship between John 20:21 and Luke 4:18-19.

   _____

   _____

   _____

   _____

   _____

   b. What do these verses say to you personally?

   _____

   _____

   _____

   _____

   _____

home study guide

LESSON THREE · DAY THREE

SECTION III

1. What has the Church been commissioned by Christ to do? Mt. 28:19-20

   _____

   _____

   _____

   _____

2. What does 2 Timothy 2:2 say to you about how the Church is to fulfill her commission from Christ?

   _____

   _____

   _____

   _____

   _____

3. What things has the Church been called to proclaim?

   _____

   _____

   _____

   _____

   _____

   _____

4. What has the Church been called to demonstrate?

   _____

   _____

   _____

   _____

5. What key role does the Holy Spirit play in the Church's work of demonstration?

   _____

   _____

   _____

   _____

home study guide

LESSON THREE · DAY FOUR

SECTION III

1. Why are the truths contained in John 15:1-8 so vital to the Church's work of demonstration?

_____

_____

_____

_____

_____

_____

_____

2. Give some references that provide us as individuals or a church with strength and encouragement as we face Satan's opposition in the work of proclaiming and demonstrating the kingdom.

_____

_____

_____

_____

_____

_____

_____

_____

3. Suggest several areas of need in your community where the church must become involved if she is to truly demonstrate God's mercy for the totality of man's fallen condition.

_____

_____

_____

_____

_____

_____

_____

_____

_____

_____

103

home study guide

LESSON THREE · DAY FIVE

SECTION IV

1. What is the significance of the fact that Jesus told the disciples to wait in Jerusalem before they went out to fulfill the commission that He had given them to go into the world?

_____

_____

_____

_____

_____

_____

2. Why was the sending of the Holy Spirit upon the Church essential to Christ's world-wide strategy? (Remember that the Spirit has come to indwell and empower *every* believer - Acts 1:8)

_____

_____

_____

_____

_____

3. What does your answer to the previous question say to you about your personal responsibility in sharing the gospel with others?

_____

_____

_____

_____

_____

4. In what ways are you personally seeking the empowering of the Holy Spirit in your own life and ministry each day?

_____

_____

_____

_____

_____

_____

LESSON FOUR - THE CHURCH: CHRIST'S BODY ON EARTH

OUTLINE

Lesson Four Update

Lesson Four Synopsis

I. **WHAT IS THE CHURCH?**
   A. The Church is Christ's Body
   B. The Church is God's Ecclesia
   C. The Church is God's Kingdom on Earth

II. **WHAT IS THE BODY OF CHRIST?**
   A. The Physical Manifestation of Christ on Earth

III. **UNDERSTANDING CHRIST'S BODY**
   A. Commentary on First Corinthians 12:12-31

IV. **THE LOCAL EXPRESSION OF CHRIST'S BODY**
   A. Diagram: Becoming the Fullness of Christ to Your
      Community
   B. Diagram Explanation

V. **SUMMATION**

Home Study Guide

Pathway of Discipleship

LESSON FOUR · THE CHURCH: CHRIST'S BODY ON EARTH

LESSON FOUR UPDATE

Lesson One   This lesson discussed God's mercy, how it was revealed in Jesus Christ and how God seeks to reproduce His deep compassion in each Christian's heart and mind. We discovered that the Christian's ministry of mercy must be wholistic in outreach to his neighbor's physical, psychological, and spiritual needs.

Lesson Two   Jesus Christ was God's mercy taking action. Through His identification with the human condition, His death, and His resurrection, God made it possible for men to step out of their impoverished condition. When we are converted, we receive inwardly the very life of Jesus Christ. This life begins, through faith, to minister to our every need. This life is able to heal the physical, social, spiritual, and any other area of our lives as well as human society. The supreme goal of this inner power is to begin to renew our minds and change them into Christ's image and character. Along with this we are able to have a foretaste of the complete restoration to come by drawing on this inner life-giving power to meet physical and temporal needs. We must be careful, however, to realize that God sovereignly ordains how much of a foretaste we are to have in this life. Paul says in Romans 8 that even we as Christians still groan with the rest of creation. We struggle as does all creation because we are living in a fallen world until the time of God's full restoration arrives. In other words, although the perfect is not yet here, God in His sovereign mercy allows us to have a small taste of His abundance in this life as we learn to apply our faith in His sovereign power.

Lesson Three   This lesson centered on the world-wide strategy of Jesus Christ. He began by personally proclaiming and demonstrating the gospel. Then He gathered twelve men and spent three years teaching and training them to carry on His ministry after He had left the earth. He then commissioned His Church to go and do as He had done, proclaim and demonstrate the gospel of God's love and mercy, making disciples of those who responded to the message. Finally, after His ascension to the Father's right hand, He sent the Holy Spirit upon the Church to empower her for the great task of proclaiming and demonstrating the kingdom throughout the earth.

LESSON FOUR · THE CHURCH: CHRIST'S BODY ON EARTH

LESSON FOUR SYNOPSIS

The Church is the body of Jesus Christ on earth. It is a group of people called together to be distinct from the world in life-style and philosophy. This group has been sent by Christ to demonstrate the principles of God's kingdom throughout the earth. The Church is literally the physical extension of Jesus Christ into this world.

According to John 7:37-39 God gives every believer Christ's life and then wills that every believer let this inner life flow from him. It is the Holy Spirit's work to see that this inner power is released to the world. Each believer is to become a channel of Christ's divine life to the world.

In this lesson we will begin to see that each believer, because of his talents, gifts, and abilities, is capable of ministering in a specific area. For some it may be ministry to people's physical needs, others may minister to psychological or social needs, while others might meet spiritual needs. All ministry, however, is Christ's life flowing forth to meet human need. The point that must be stressed is that the fullness of Christ can only be totally ministered to all men when the Church becomes effective as Christ's body. This means that every believer must function and flow under the Head who is Jesus Christ. *God wills that every local Church fully become everything that Jesus Christ would be to the community if He were there in bodily form.*

The individual believer and the Church as a whole must view the world with the deep compassion and pity of God who dwells within them. In turn, each believer and the Church must actively minister the life of Christ to the needs of the world.

LESSON FOUR · THE CHURCH: CHRIST'S BODY ON EARTH

I. WHAT IS THE CHURCH?

I. WHAT IS THE CHURCH?

A. The Church is Christ's Body

The local church is to be everything to the community it serves that Jesus Christ would be if He were there in physical form. This is the predominate theme of this lesson and the rest of *Pathway 103*.

B. The Church is God's Ecclesia

Ecclesia is the word for church in the Greek New Testament. It means "those who are called out" and it originally referred to a meeting of all the citizens of Athens called out or called together to discuss the affairs of state. The Church is a called-out body of people separate in character and distinct in philosophy from the world around them. (This point will be discussed in depth under, "Blessed are the pure in heart" in *Pathway 104.*)

C. The Church is God's Kingdom on Earth

The Church is a group of people who have submitted themselves to God's rightful authority as the ruler of the universe. The Church, therefore, is a kingdom, an organized community under Christ, her heavenly King. As such, the Church demonstrates to the world what things are like when God is given His rightful place in the hearts of individuals as well as in society. The Church is a collective witness to the world of what God's kingdom is like. (This point will be further expanded under, "Blessed are the peacemakers" in *Pathway 104.*)

II. WHAT IS THE BODY OF CHRIST?

A. The Physical Manifestation of Christ on Earth

The Church is a dynamic extension of the on-going ministry of Jesus Christ on earth. Men can only see Christ when they are touched by the living Church of God.

1. As has been stated in Lesson 2, when Jesus Christ was here in bodily form, He was the exact expression or representation of God to every person He met.

LESSON FOUR · THE CHURCH: CHRIST'S BODY ON EARTH

II. WHAT IS THE BODY OF CHRIST?

Colossians 1:19
For God was pleased to have all his fullness dwell in him.

Romans 12:5-8
So in Christ we who are many form one body, and each member belongs to all the others. ⁶We have different gifts, according to the grace given us. If a man's gift is prophesying, let him use it in proportion to his faith. ⁷If it is serving, let him serve; if it is teaching, let him teach; ⁸if it is encouraging, let him encourage; if it is contributing to the needs of others, let him give generously; if it is leadership, let him govern diligently; if it is showing mercy, let him do it cheerfully.

Ephesians 1:22-23
And God placed all things under his feet and appointed him to be head over everything for the church, ²³which is his body, the fullness of him who fills everything in every way.

2. Colossians 1:19 says He was also the fullness of God. He was fully and completely God and, therefore, He was able to meet man's needs totally.

3. No man before or since has ever been the fullness of God. Only in Jesus Christ did all spiritual gifts (equipment to meet every occasion and need) dwell.

4. Only the Church collective (when all anointed talents and spiritual gifts are flowing from each member) can become all that Christ would be to the world and more if He were here in bodily form (Ro. 12:5-8; Eph. 1:22-23).

5. The Church has the potential of accomplishing more than Jesus accomplished, because now His Spirit is not confined to one physical body. The Spirit of Christ is now everywhere through His extended body, the Church.

6. William Barclay has commented on the truth of the body of Christ:

> There is a tremendous thought here. Christ is no longer in this world in the body; and therefore if he wants a task done within the world he has to find a man to do it. If he wants a child taught, he has to find a teacher to teach him; if he wants a sick person cured, he has to find a physician or surgeon to do his work; if he wants his story told, he has to find a man to tell it. Literally, we have to be the body of Christ, hands to do his work, feet to run upon his errands, a voice to speak for him.
>
> *"He has no hands but our hands*
> *To do His work today;*
> *He has no feet but our feet*
> *To lead men in His way;*
> *He has no voice but our voice*
> *To tell men how He died;*
> *He has no help but our help*
> *To lead them to His side."*
>
> Here is the supreme glory of the Christian man—he is part of the body of Christ upon earth.[1]

---

[1] William Barclay, *The Letters to the Corinthians,* (The Westminster Press, 1956), pp. 113-114.

LESSON FOUR · THE CHURCH: CHRIST'S BODY ON EARTH

III. UNDERSTANDING CHRIST'S BODY

Luke 4:18-19
"The Spirit of the Lord is on me, because he has anointed me to preach good news to the poor.
He has sent me to proclaim freedom for the prisoners and recovery of sight for the blind,
to release the oppressed,
19 to proclaim the year of the Lord's favor."

John 17:4
I have brought you glory on earth by completing the work you gave me to do.

John 17:22
I have given them the glory that you gave me, that they may be one as we are one.

John 15:1
"I am the true vine and my Father is the gardener."

7. We must keep in mind that God has called His Church, this extended body, to carry on the ministry which His Son began, the ministry of Luke 4:18-19 (See Lesson 3, Section I, A).

8. The body of Christ collectively is to become the total expression of God's character to the world. When the worldly man looks upon the Church, he is to see God—His mercy, His purity, and His love going to any depths to help, restore, heal, deliver, and redeem a helpless and hopeless humanity. The Church (when every member is functioning) is the only hope for fallen man's wretched condition this side of Christ's return.

9. The Church then (more specifically each local church with all its various spiritual gifts functioning) is the living embodiment of Jesus Christ to the world.

III. UNDERSTANDING CHRIST'S BODY

A. Commentary on First Corinthians 12:12-31

1. Verse 12: "The body is a unit, though it is made up of many parts; and though all its parts are many, they form one body. So it is with Christ."

Comment: The body of Christ, although it is made up of many individual members, is still only one body. The Church is Christ in the world. As Christ was the expression of the Father's glory, the Church is to express the glory and character of the Son (Jn. 17:4, 22).

2. Verse 13: "For we were all baptized by one Spirit into one body—whether Jews or Greeks, slave or free—and we were all given the one Spirit to drink."

Comment: All of us are born of the same Spirit and have been made members of the same body. We are all like branches attached to the same vine (Jn. 15:1). Individually, we are to be a portion of Christ's

LESSON FOUR · THE CHURCH: CHRIST'S BODY ON EARTH

III. UNDERSTANDING CHRIST'S BODY

mercy to a hurting world. Collectively, we become the sum of all that He seeks to accomplish in the restoration of fallen man.

3. Verses 14-20: "Now the body is not made up of one part but of many. If the foot should say, 'Because I am not a hand, I do not belong to the body,' it would not for that reason cease to be part of the body. And if the ear should say, 'Because I am not an eye, I do not belong to the body,' it would not for that reason cease to be part of the body. If the whole body were an eye, where would the sense of hearing be? If the whole body were an ear, where would the sense of smell be? But in fact God has arranged the parts in the body, every one of them, just as he wanted them to be. If they were all one part, where would the body be? As it is, there are many parts, but one body."

Comment: The body of Christ is ineffectual unless every member is functioning, and there is a blending of various gifts under one Head. Here, possibly, is where the Church has often struggled the most. First, a relatively small percentage (15%) have discovered their spiritual gifts. These verses indicate one of these reasons for this situation. Some feel their gifts are not important or useful and therefore, they do not really consider themselves part of the body. Paul points out, however, that all the parts are important to the proper functioning of the whole and that it is God Himself who has assigned each member its function. The diversity of gifts in the body is essential to its very existence.

4. Verses 21-26: "The eye cannot say to the hand, 'I don't need you!' And the head cannot say to the feet, 'I don't need you!' On the contrary, those parts of the

LESSON FOUR · THE CHURCH: CHRIST'S BODY ON EARTH

III. UNDERSTANDING CHRIST'S BODY

body that seem to be weaker are indispensable, and the parts that we think are less honorable we treat with special honor. And the parts that are unpresentable are treated with special modesty, while our presentable parts need no special treatment. But God has combined the members of the body and has given greater honor to the parts that lacked it, so that there should be no division in the body, but that its parts should have equal concern for each other. If one part suffers, every part suffers with it; if one part is honored, every part rejoices with it.''

Comment: All members are important and all have something to contribute. The world, and to a great extent, the Corinthian church, minimized the role of people who did not possess the charisma to be out front. How typical this is of society's approach, but how dreadful it is when the same attitude exists in the local church. The Corinthians had been emphasizing the importance of those people who were being used extensively in one of the nine supernatural manifestations of the Holy Spirit (vv. 8-10). The great bulk of the people felt unneeded and insignificant because the more practical roles were not emphasized as being important. There were even those who tried to exclude others from the body because they did not have any ''important gifts.'' Here is where our independent natures struggle with maintaining unity and submission one to another. Only when all gifts are functioning and each individual is able to blend under the direction of the whole can we approach being all that God desires us to be in our local Christian communities. All must realize that the one who types or sews or feeds is as much an expression of God's Spirit as one who prophesies.

5. Verses 27-30: ''Now you are the body of Christ, and each one of you is a part of it. And in

LESSON FOUR · THE CHURCH: CHRIST'S BODY ON EARTH

III. UNDERSTANDING CHRIST'S BODY

the church God has appointed first of all apostles, second prophets, third teachers, then workers of miracles, also those having gifts of healing, those able to help others, those with gifts of administration, and those speaking in different kinds of tongues. Are all apostles? Are all prophets? Are all teachers? Do all work miracles? Do all have gifts of healing? Do all speak in tongues? Do all interpret?''

Comment: There are literally hundreds of gifts in the body of Christ. There are the gifts of leadership: apostles, prophets, teachers; but are all apostles, prophets and teachers? The answer is clear: of course not. There are many others serving as helpers or administrators who are just as important.

6. Verse 31: "But earnestly desire the greater gifts. And now I will show you the most excellent way.''

Comment: There is some ambiguity in the meaning of the Greek text and, therefore, in the interpretation of this verse. It is also possible to translate this verse as follows: "But you (meaning the Corinthians) are earnestly desiring (or seeking) the best gifts. And yet I will show you a still more excellent way.''

If such a rendering were the case, it would give more meaning to what Paul has been trying to say in 1 Corinthians chapter 12, and what he is about to say in 1 Corinthians chapter 13.

The Corinthians thought that some gifts were better than others and it was these gifts that they were earnestly seeking. Paul says, however, the most important thing is not the nature of your gifts—God has already determined that (v. 18)—but rather, the way in which they should be exercised: the way of love.

Pathway of Discipleship

LESSON FOUR - THE CHURCH: CHRIST'S BODY ON EARTH

IV. THE LOCAL EXPRESSION OF CHRIST'S BODY

IV. THE LOCAL EXPRESSION OF CHRIST'S BODY

A. Diagram:

BECOMING THE FULLNESS OF CHRIST TO YOUR COMMUNITY

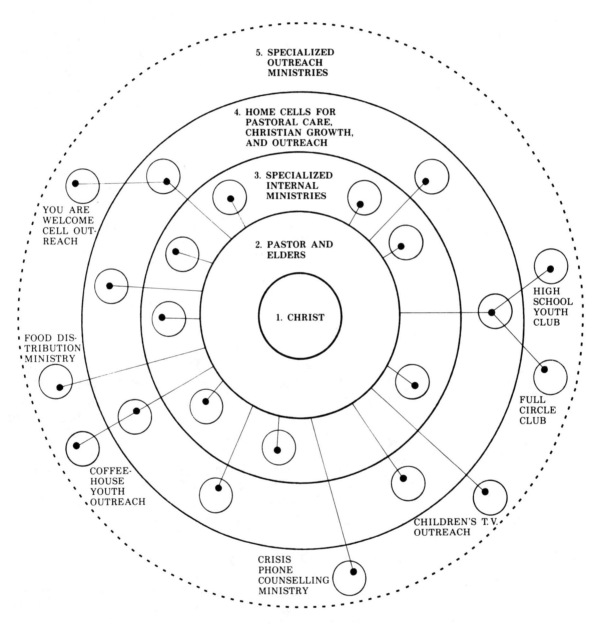

- ● Cell leader or deacon in charge of a specific ministry.
- ◯ A. Home cell.
  B. Ministry cell made up of people committed to a specific ministry.
- _____ Line of responsibility and accountability.

LESSON FOUR · THE CHURCH: CHRIST'S BODY ON EARTH

IV. THE LOCAL EXPRESSION OF CHRIST'S BODY

B. Diagram Explanation:

BECOMING THE FULLNESS OF CHRIST TO YOUR COMMUNITY

1. Circles 1 and 2—The local church leadership under Christ

   a. Christ is the Head of the Church and seeks to lead His people through the vision of the pastor and elders of each local church.

   b. God will usually give the vision to the pastor.

   c. Elders are to seek God's will in prayer with the pastor to determine the details of this vision as well as the when and how of making it a reality.

2. Circle 3—Specialized Internal Ministries

   a. The circles inside circle 3 tied by spokes to the eldership represent specialized pastoral ministries in the body. Their purpose is to meet specific needs within the local body of believers. Examples would include ministry to church families, children, youth, senior citizens, and so forth.

   b. Each one of these ministries is administered or headed by a deacon, deaconness, or pastoral assistant, depending on the scope of the ministry involved.

   c. Each deacon or pastor in charge of such a ministry is responsible to the eldership of the church.

3. Circle 4—Home Cells for Pastoral Care, Christian Growth, and Outreach

   a. Each believer should meet in a weekly cell for study, fellowship, body ministry, and prayer. This is a key context for Christian growth.

   b. This cell, headed by a deacon or deaconness in charge, becomes a unit of care and concern one for another. It is here that the believer finds the needs of the body, soul, and spirit being met. This is where pastoral care takes place most effectively.

IV. THE LOCAL EXPRESSION OF CHRIST'S BODY

c. This cell also has an evangelistic function. The home cell often is the first point of contact between the non-Christian and the local body. People often come to Christ either in the home cell or as a result of further contact with its members.

4. Circle 5—Specialized Outreach Ministries

a. First, there are specialized outreaches headed by deacons, deaconnesses, or full-time assistants who are responsible directly to the eldership such as:

(1) Food distribution ministry to the needy families in the community.

(2) Children's T. V. outreach.

(3) Crisis phone counselling ministry.

b. Second, individual home cells should of themselves take on group outreach efforts such as:

(1) *You Are Welcome:* An evangelistic cell group booklet that provides a method whereby neighbors are introduced to the gospel.

(2) Full Circle Clubs: A children's Bible club method through which bridges are built in the community and to the homes of the children involved.

(3) High school youth clubs, coffeehouse youth outreaches or any other creative evangelistic activities.

Acts 2:42
They devoted themselves to the apostles' teaching and to the fellowship, to the breaking of bread and to prayer.

Acts 2:46-47
Every day they continued to meet together in the temple courts. They broke bread in their homes and ate together with glad and sincere hearts, [47] praising God and enjoying the favor of all the people. And the Lord added to their number daily those who were being saved.

5. The entire body comes together once a week to hear the pastor's teaching and instruction. They also meet in homes to minister one to another and to give and receive spiritual edification and pastoral care (Acts 2:42, 46-47). The early church met collectively (in the temple) and in small groups (house to house).

V. SUMMATION

1. The Church is literally the body of Jesus Christ on earth. She is God's ecclesia, a body of people called out from the world to a new holy philosophy and life-style which conforms to God's character and truth.

2. The Church is also the kingdom of God on earth. She is the place where God is allowed to rule as king. The Church, therefore, is a model to society of what life is like when God is given His rightful place in people's lives.

3. The Church is the physical presence of Christ on this earth. She is an extension of the Incarnation. The Church is the only way that Jesus Christ can now express Himself to mankind in concrete words and actions.

4. Although the Church is made up of many different members with differing gifts and functions, she forms one unified body. Each member is essential to the proper functioning of the whole. The Church, therefore, is only effective when each member has discovered his or her spiritual gift, developed it, and put it to use in the body.

5. Christ wants every local church to be all that He is to their community. This can be done as a church structures itself to provide for the continuing nurture and pastoral care of its members as well as an ongoing ministry to the physical, social, and spiritual needs of its community.

103

home study guide

LESSON FOUR · DAY ONE

SECTIONS I · II

1. Using Ephesians 1:22-23, describe the concept of the Church as the body of Christ.

_____

_____

_____

_____

_____

2. Using the following verses, explain the concept of the Church as God's ecclesia. Eph. 5:1-14; Col. 1:13-14; 1 Pet. 2:9-10.

_____

_____

_____

_____

_____

_____

3. List two or three scriptures that refer to the kingdom of God and use them to write a brief explanation of how the Church is actually God's kingdom on earth.

_____

_____

_____

_____

_____

4. What correlation between the teaching of Colossians 1:19 and 1 Corinthians 12:12-14, 27-30 with reference to the role of the Church on earth is suggested in Lesson 4?

_____

_____

_____

_____

_____

5. How is it that the Church has the potential of accomplishing more than Jesus did in His earthly ministry?

_____

_____

_____

103

home study guide

LESSON FOUR · DAY TWO

SECTION III

1. Read 1 Corinthians 12:27-31 as well as Romans 12:4-8 and 1 Peter 4:10-11, and make a list of all the spiritual gifts that you discover in these three portions of Scripture.

_____

_____

_____

_____

_____

_____

_____

2. Read 1 Corinthians 12:4-11 and Ephesians 4:11 and list the additional spiritual gifts that you find in these two passages.

_____

_____

_____

_____

_____

_____

_____

3. Analyze all the spiritual gifts that you have listed above. See if there are some repeats, and list the number of gifts mentioned in the New Testament.

_____

_____

_____

4. Are the nine supernatural gifts mentioned in 1 Corinthians 12:4-11 different in importance from any of the gifts mentioned in other portions of Scripture? Why or why not?

_____

_____

_____

_____

_____

_____

_____

home study guide

LESSON FOUR · DAY THREE

SECTION III

Carefully study 1 Corinthians 12:12-31 in more than one Bible version in order to answer the following questions:

1. What gives unity to the many different members of Christ's body? vv. 12-14

_____

2. a. What were some of the Corinthians saying about their spiritual gifts? vv. 14-19

_____

_____

   b. What does Paul tell them? _____

_____

3. a. What were some of the Corinthians saying about people's spiritual gifts? vv. 21-25

_____

_____

   b. What does Paul tell them? _____

_____

4. Why should there be no divisions in the body of Christ? vv. 21-25 _____

_____

_____

5. What point is Paul trying to make with the series of questions (all of which expect a negative response) in vv. 29-30? See also verses 17 and 19.

_____

_____

_____

6. Are some gifts and ministries more important than others in the local church? Why or why not?

_____

_____

_____

7. List those gifts and ministries that we in the modern church sometimes make the mistake of considering more important than any others.

_____

_____

_____

8. Can one individual totally minister Christ's life to every human need? Explain your answer using this passage in First Corinthians.

_____

_____

_____

103

home study guide

LESSON FOUR - DAYS FOUR & FIVE

SECTION IV

1. Study the diagram in your notes entitled: "Becoming the Fullness of Christ to Your Community." Redraw the diagram or use the diagram in your notes, and begin to fill in the various circles with ministries you would like to see functioning in your local church. For instance, in circle 3, list all of the specialized internal ministries that you feel your church should be involved in relative to children, the elderly, and so forth. In circle 5, list the various specialized ministries and outreaches that you would like to see your church involved in.

2. Please read thoroughly the reasons for corporate worship, for specialized ministries, for home cell groups, and for outreach from both cells and the local church found in section IV, B. Be ready to share with your group what this means to you in your understanding of the local church.

   a. What is the purpose of corporate worship and teaching?

   _____

   _____

   _____

   _____

   b. What is the purpose of a weekly home cell group?

   _____

   _____

   _____

   c. How do specialized ministries support individual concern for human need?

   _____

   _____

   _____

   d. How can doctors, dentists, psychologists and all types of professionals become a part of a specialized outreach ministry of the church?

   _____

   _____

   _____

   e. How can cells reach out to help in the work of evangelism? (Please share your own concepts.)

   _____

   _____

   _____

LESSON FIVE · UNDERSTANDING SPIRITUAL GIFTS

OUTLINE

Lesson Five Update

Lesson Five Synopsis

I. SPIRITUAL GIFTS AND GRACE
A. Charisma
B. Spiritual Gift

II. THREE KINDS OF GIFTS
A. Support Gifts
B. Motivational Gifts
C. Supernatural Gifts

III. DIFFERENT GIFTS, MINISTRIES, AND WORKINGS
A. First Corinthians 12:4-6
B. Gifts
C. Ministries
D. Workings
E. Diagram
F. Diagram Commentary

IV. MINISTERING GOD'S GRACE
A. First Peter 4:10
B. God's Free Gift

V. MATURITY INCREASES EFFECTIVENESS
A. Maturity: An On-going Work
B. Equipping Through Experience

VI. OVERVIEW

VII. SUMMATION

Home Study Guide

Lesson One   We discovered how God views mankind and how He is changing His children to view the world and feel for the world as He does.

Lesson Two   We discovered how Jesus Christ was the fulfillment of God's mercy and love. He was God's mercy taking action. Through His work on Calvary and His resurrection, Jesus Christ gave back to man the creative life of God. This creative life promises healing for the whole man, but this healing will not come to completion until Jesus Christ returns.

Lesson Three   Here we learned that Jesus poured His life into twelve men who could carry on His ministry after He left as well as train others to do the same. He commissioned His Church to carry the gospel to the world and empowered her to do this by sending the Holy Spirit.

Lesson Four   We learned how the Church is Christ's body on earth, the continuation of His ministry to the whole world. The Church is actually the physical manifestation of Christ in the world bringing His message of the kingdom and ministering His divine life.

This lesson will begin to explain more fully how Jesus Christ expresses Himself through His body, the Church.

To each believer Christ gives the spiritual gifts needed to fulfill His purposes. To some, usually those in so-called full-time ministry, He gives supportive leadership gifts. These gifts mentioned in Ephesians 4:11 are to equip the saints and provide an essential structure that supports the body, feeds it, and prompts its growth.

To each believer He gives one of the motivational gifts mentioned in Romans chapter 12. These gifts prompt believers to work in different areas and do the various things He wants done.

Finally, we will discover that each believer has within him the Holy Spirit who gives nine supernatural gifts to the Church. These gifts mentioned in 1 Corinthians chapter 12, equip the Church to carry on the supernatural aspect of Christ's ministry on earth.

The Holy Spirit seeks to work through the total personality of the believer. This means that your temperament, abilities, training, creativity, experience, and so forth will all play a part in determining what area of ministry you will be involved in.

No matter what aspect of ministry your gift may involve you in, it is important to realize that you are called to freely minister God's grace (the blessings of His kingdom) to people. A key factor that will determine how effective you are in doing this is the degree of your maturity in Christ.

LESSON FIVE · UNDERSTANDING SPIRITUAL GIFTS

I. SPIRITUAL GIFTS AND GRACE

Romans 12:6
We have different gifts, according to the grace given us. If a man's gift is prophesying, let him use it in proportion to his faith.

1 Peter 4:10
Each one should use whatever gift he has received to serve others, faithfully administering God's grace in its various forms.

1 Timothy 4:14
Do not neglect your gift, which was given you through a prophetic message when the body of elders laid their hands on you.

Ephesians 4:11
It was he who gave some to be apostles, some to be prophets, some to be evangelists, and some to be pastors and teachers.

I. SPIRITUAL GIFTS AND GRACE

A. Charisma

Charisma is the Greek word used throughout the New Testament to describe spiritual gifts.

1. Paul says every believer has his own *charisma* according to the grace of God given to him (Ro. 12:6).

2. Peter says every man should serve others using the *charisma* or gift he has received from God (1 Pet. 4:10).

3. Timothy was never to neglect the *charisma* that came to him at the laying on of hands by the presbytery (1 Tim. 4:14).

4. William Barclay says regarding *charisma:*

> The whole basic idea of the word is that of a free and undeserved gift, of something given to a man unearned and unmerited, something which comes from God's grace and which could never have been achieved or attained or possessed by a man's own effort.[1]

B. Spiritual Gift

1. A spiritual gift is something God freely gives, not because it is earned, but because He chooses to give it.

2. These gifts find fuller expression as the individual matures and develops in God.

II. THREE KINDS OF GIFTS

God gives freely and without favor three types of gifts to His children.

A. Support Gifts

1. To some he gives gifts of support and leadership (Eph. 4:11):

a. Apostles

These were the ones personally commissioned by Christ to found the Church. Their ministry continues to come to us through their writings in the

---

[1] William Barclay, *New Testament Words* (The Westminster Press, 1974), p. 63.

II. THREE KINDS OF GIFTS

New Testament. In a secondary sense, the gift of apostleship is operational today in those who found new churches or work in areas previously untouched by the gospel. Those with an apostlic gift lay the basic foundational structure upon which others build the local church.

b. Prophets

These individuals are gifted to vigorously emphasize a particular aspect of God's truth to His people at a timely moment.

c. Evangelists

These are people with a special gift of winning others, usually in large numbers, to Christ. They are called to proclaim the gospel and to equip others to do the same.

d. Pastors

The pastor is called to continually nourish and protect the local body of believers.

e. Teachers

This gift is part of the pastoral gift because a pastor must be able to teach. There are also those, however, who may not serve in a strictly pastoral function but assist the pastor in building up the body of Christ through the ministry of teaching.

The body of Christ builds upon the ministry of the people who possess these supportive leadership gifts. These gifts are indispensable to the growth and life of both the local as well as the world-wide Church of Jesus Christ.

2. Gifts of support and leadership are given to relatively few people. They are given because of the call of God to certain individuals for full-time ministry. These gifts do not find full expression until spiritual maturity is developed in the individual.

LESSON FIVE · UNDERSTANDING SPIRITUAL GIFTS

II. THREE KINDS OF GIFTS

3. There are many within the body of Christ who are called to assist in these support ministries. For example:

   a. God may call you to be part of a pioneer church, assisting in the work of apostleship which involves building a solid foundation for a new local body of believers.

   b. God may give you a prophetic insight into the needs of the church. This usually goes hand-in-hand with the ministry of intercessory prayer.

   c. Your calling may be evangelism and so you will become involved in some type of evangelistic outreach from the local church. It should be noted that although not everyone has an evangelistic ministry, all are called to give verbal witness of their faith.

   d. God's call may be one of assisting in the pastoral care of the body. Quite often a home cell or small group leader serves in this capacity.

   e. Those with the teaching motivation and gift are called to share in the teaching and equipping ministry of the Church.

B. Motivational Gifts

Romans 12:6-8
We have different gifts, according to the grace given us. If a man's gift is prophesying, let him use it in proportion to his faith. [7]If it is serving, let him serve; if it is teaching, let him teach; [8]if it is encouraging, let him encourage; if it is contributing to the needs of others, let him give generously; if it is leadership, let him govern diligently; if it is showing mercy, let him do it cheerfully.

1. To all believers a predominant and specific gift of motivation is given. These gifts, which are found in Romans 12:6-8, can be briefly defined as follows:

   a. *Prophecy* The ability to declare God's truth which touches the heart and brings conviction.

   b. *Serving* The ability to show love by meeting the practical needs of others.

   c. *Teaching* The ability to clarify truth after thorough study and research.

II. THREE KINDS OF GIFTS

d. *Exhortation* The ability to encourage others to grow spiritually, even in the face of hardship and suffering.

e. *Giving* The ability to contribute generously of financial and material resources for the Lord's work.

f. *Administration* The ability to coordinate people, resources, and schedules to achieve goals.

g. *Mercy* The ability to identify with and comfort those in distress.

2. One of these motivational gifts dominates each person's way of doing things in the body of Christ. Jesus Christ possesses all of these gifts. In His body, however, these qualities are distributed among its members. When combined, these gifts motivate people to meet every need in the body of Christ and in the world. The use of these gifts depends upon a person's commitment. For this reason, many needs fail to be met because people are not sufficiently committed or do not respond to the Spirit's desire within them to develop and utilize their gifts to God's glory. In Lessons 7 and 8, the concept of motivational gifts will be explained more fully.

3. The Holy Spirit chooses to work through the committed individual in a certain predominant way based upon that individual's personality. One individual may be used predominantly in an intuitive or prophetic way while another may be used predominantly in a serving way. This is not to say that God, the Holy Spirit, will not prompt a person to be merciful, even though their major motivational gift is teaching. The key to understanding motivational gifts lies in the word, "predominant."

C. Supernatural Gifts

1. First Corinthians 12:7-10 lists for us the nine supernatural gifts of the Holy Spirit:

1 Corinthians 12:7-10
Now to each one the manifestation of the Spirit

LESSON FIVE · UNDERSTANDING SPIRITUAL GIFTS

II. THREE KINDS OF GIFTS

is given for the common good. [8]To one there is given through the Spirit the message of wisdom, to another the message of knowledge by means of the same Spirit, [9]to another faith by the same Spirit, to another gifts of healing by that one Spirit, [10]to another miraculous powers, to another prophecy, to another the ability to distinguish between spirits, to another the ability to speak in different kinds of tongues, and to still another the interpretation of tongues.

John 14:11-12
Believe me when I say that I am in the Father and the Father is in me; or at least believe on the evidence of the miracles themselves. [12]I tell you the truth, anyone who has faith in me will do what I have been doing. He will do even greater things than these, because I am going to the Father.

1 Corinthians 12:11
All these are the work of one and the same Spirit, and he gives them to each one, just as he determines.

Acts 8:5-7
Philip went down to a city in Samaria and proclaimed the Christ there. [6]When the crowds heard Philip and saw the miraculous signs he did, they all paid close attention to what he said. [7]With shrieks, evil spirits came out of many, and many paralytics and cripples were healed.

Acts 11:15-18
"As I began to speak, the Holy Spirit came on them as he had come on us at the beginning. [16]Then I remembered what the Lord had said, 'John baptized with water, but you will be baptized with the Holy Spirit.' [17]So if God gave them the same gift as he gave us, who believed in the Lord Jesus Christ, who was I to think that I could oppose God!'"
[18]When they heard this, they had no further objections and praised God, saying, "So then, God has even granted the Gentiles repentance unto life."

a. The word of wisdom.

b. The word of knowledge.

c. The gift of faith.

d. Gifts of healing.

e. Working of miracles.

f. Prophecy.

g. Discerning of spirits.

h. Unknown tongues.

i. Interpretation of tongues.

These gifts are the supernatural expression of Jesus Christ through His body. They allow His Church on earth to carry on His supernatural ministry. This means that His body is fully equipped to do all that He did while He was on earth (Jn. 14:11-12).

2. The supernatural gifts of the Holy Spirit reside in the Holy Spirit Himself, who lives in the heart of every believer. The Holy Spirit is the one who decides to use certain people in certain gifts on certain occasions.

3. The Scripture says that the Lord gives these supernatural gifts, "to each one, just as He determines" (1 Cor. 12:11). How God chooses to express Himself supernaturally depends upon the calling of the individual as well as the circumstances of time and place involved in each situation.

a. For example, the gifts of healing, working of miracles, and discerning of spirits in the New Testament were predominantly associated with the gift of the evangelist (Acts 8:5-7).

b. The word of wisdom and word of knowledge are often associated with the administrative, pastoral, and teaching ministries of the church.

(1) In Acts 11:15-18 we learn that Peter came into a fuller understanding of the universal scope of the gospel—it even included the Gentiles—through a word of knowledge from the Holy Spirit reminding him of the teaching of Christ.

LESSON FIVE · UNDERSTANDING SPIRITUAL GIFTS

III. DIFFERENT GIFTS, MINISTRIES, AND WORKINGS

Acts 15:25-29
So we all agreed to choose some men and send them to you with our dear friends Barnabas and Paul—²⁶men who have risked their lives for the name of our Lord Jesus Christ. ²⁷Therefore we are sending Judas and Silas to confirm by word of mouth what we are writing. ²⁸It seemed good to the Holy Spirit and to us not to burden you with anything beyond the following requirements: ²⁹You are to abstain from food sacrificed to idols, from blood, from the meat of strangled animals and from sexual immorality. You will do well to avoid these things.

1 Corinthians 14:5
I would like every one of you to speak in tongues, but I would rather have you prophesy. He who prophesies is greater than one who speaks in tongues, unless he interprets, so that the church may be edified.

1 Corinthians 14:26
What then shall we say, brothers? When you come together, everyone has a hymn, or a word of instruction, a revelation, a tongue or an interpretation. All of these must be done for the strengthening of the church.

(2) In Acts 15:25-29 the council at Jerusalem wrote to the churches and shared with them a word of wisdom from the Holy Spirit that had come forth during their deliberations.

c. The gift of tongues, interpretation of tongues and prophecy, according to 1 Corinthians 14, is associated with the public worship service (1 Cor. 14:5, 26).

d. Every believer should be available to be used by the Holy Spirit at any time. There may be situations where you will be used in a supernatural gift of the Holy Spirit even though you are not normally accustomed to being used in this way. If you are in the right place at the right time and are open to the Holy Spirit, He will use you.

III. DIFFERENT GIFTS, MINISTRIES, AND WORKINGS

A. First Corinthians 12:4-6:

There are different kinds of (spiritual) gifts but the same Spirit. There are different kinds of service (ministries), but the same Lord. There are different kinds of working, but the same God works all of them in all men.

B. Gifts

As stated under section II above, there are three types of spiritual gifts:

1. Support or Leadership Gifts (Eph. 4:11).
2. Motivational Gifts (Ro. 12:6-8).
3. Supernatural Gifts (1 Cor. 12:8-10).

C. Ministries (Services)

1. There are many hundreds of ministries or avenues of service expression in the body of Christ. The avenue of ministry may be one person or numerous people working together to provide a needed service or outreach to the local body or community.

LESSON FIVE · UNDERSTANDING SPIRITUAL GIFTS

III. DIFFERENT GIFTS, MINISTRIES, AND WORKINGS

Acts 6:1-7
In those days when the number of disciples was increasing, the Grecian Jews among them complained against those of the Aramaic-speaking community because their widows were being overlooked in the daily distribution of food. [2]So the Twelve gathered all the disciples together and said, "It would not be right for us to neglect the ministry of the word of God in order to wait on tables. [3]Brothers, choose seven men from among you who are known to be full of the Spirit and wisdom. We will turn this responsibility over to them [4]and will give our attention to prayer and the ministry of the word."
[5]This proposal pleased the whole group. They chose Stephen, a man full of faith and of the Holy Spirit; also Philip, Procorus, Nicanor, Timon, Parmenas, and Nicolas from Antioch, a convert to Judaism. [6]They presented these men to the apostles, who prayed and laid their hands on them.
[7]So the word of God spread. The number of disciples in Jerusalem increased rapidly, and a large number of priests became obedient to the faith.

Ephesians 4:11-12
It was he who gave some to be apostles, some to be prophets, some to be evangelists, and some to be pastors and teachers, [12]to prepare God's people for works of service, so that the body of Christ may be built up.

2. Examples of Ministries:

   a. The first deacons performed a ministry to the widows, orphans, and needy of the Jerusalem church (Acts 6:1-7).

   b. Teaching Sunday School.

   c. Ushering.

   d. Volunteer labor on a church building.

   e. Visiting shut-ins.

3. All Christians are being equipped for the work of service or ministry (Eph. 4:11-12). Each person should be part of some ministry to the body or ministry outreach to the lost and needy people in the community.

4. As the local church expands its leadership base through discipleship training, more and more ministries will spring up as individuals mature in Christ and desire to take on responsibility. The church must then provide avenues of service and ministry expression for these individuals.

5. Most often it is the pastor who feels the need to reach out in new, undeveloped areas of ministry.

   a. The first step in developing new areas is to find a lay person of deacon or deaconess qualifications with the natural abilities to lead in that area. Such a person must then be recommended to the pastor and the eldership.

   b. If such a person cannot be found, then a pastor is expanding too fast. Refer to the diagrams showing the need for developing a leadership base in *Pathway 101,* Lesson 3, Section III.

   c. Once the qualified person has been identified, he or she, under pastoral direction, should then recruit others who have the spiritual gifts and talents necessary to develop that new area of ministry.

III. DIFFERENT GIFTS, MINISTRIES, AND WORKINGS

6. God may place a desire within a lay person to reach out in undeveloped area of service. If that person has deacon or deaconess qualifications (see *Pathway 102*, Lesson 5) and the necessary administrative abilities, then the eldership should be open to launching out in faith with the individual in that new area of ministry.

   a. The pastor and eldership in the local church should be constantly open to move in faith as such individuals are called by God.

   b. Laymen who are called by God to open new doors of service should submit their vision to the pastor and eldership for consideration and should be patient until the eldership feels that it is time to move in the given direction.

7. There are other ministries or works of service that simply need to be done. These ministries, which involve only one individual, may not always need approval from the pastor.

   a. Examples:

      (1) Visiting the sick.
      (2) Giving rides to church.
      (3) Having new people into your home.

   b. It is good, however, to let the pastor know what you are doing so he knows you are part of the ministry outreach of the local body. This will help the pastor direct others your way who are in need of such a service.

8. Any ministry that develops into a structure involving more than one individual should be submitted to the local church leadership.

D. Workings

1. Each person is a distinct and unique individual. His natural God-given abilities, talents, and resources differ from all other people. As a result, God chooses to work differently in and through each individual.

LESSON FIVE · UNDERSTANDING SPIRITUAL GIFTS

III. DIFFERENT GIFTS, MINISTRIES, AND WORKINGS

2. According to the Parable of the Talents in Matthew 25:14-30, not everyone is of equal ability. Based upon their greater abilities, some are given more opportunities than others. However, all are equally responsible for the stewardship and effective use of the natural endowments entrusted to them.

(Section III continues with the diagram on the next page.)

LESSON FIVE · UNDERSTANDING SPIRITUAL GIFTS

III. DIFFERENT GIFTS, MINISTRIES, AND WORKINGS

E. Diagram: **GOD'S WORKINGS THROUGH THE TOTAL PERSON**

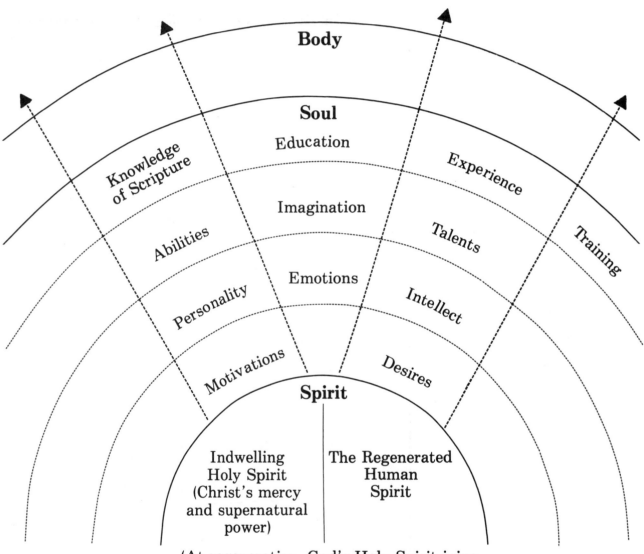

The dotted lines and arrows represent the Holy Spirit working through the total person to minister Christ's mercy to the world.

LESSON FIVE · UNDERSTANDING SPIRITUAL GIFTS

III. DIFFERENT GIFTS, MINISTRIES, AND WORKINGS

1 Corinthians 12:6-7
There are different kinds of working, but the same God works all of them in all men. ⁷Now to each one the manifestation of the Spirit is given for the common good.

Romans 8:9-16
You, however, are controlled not by the sinful nature but by the Spirit, if the Spirit of God lives in you. And if anyone does not have the Spirit of Christ, he does not belong to Christ. ¹⁰But if Christ is in you, your body is dead because of sin, yet your spirit is alive because of righteousness. ¹¹And if the Spirit of him who raised Jesus from the dead is living in you, he who raised Christ from the dead will also give life to your mortal bodies through his Spirit, who lives in you. ¹²Therefore, brothers, we have an obligation —but it is not to the sinful nature, to live according to it. ¹³For if you live according to the sinful nature, you will die; but if by the Spirit you put to death the misdeeds of the body, you will live, ¹⁴because those who are led by the Spirit of God are sons of God. ¹⁵For you did not receive a spirit that makes you a slave again to fear, but you received the Spirit of sonship. And by him we cry, "*Abba,* Father." ¹⁶The Spirit himself testifies with our spirit that we are God's children.

1 Corinthians 12:11
All these are the work of one and the same Spirit, and he gives them to each man, just as he determines.

Colossians 2:9
For in Christ all the fullness of the Deity lives in bodily form.

F. Diagram Commentary: God's Workings Through the Total Person

1. First Corinthians 12:6-7:

   There are many ways in which God works in our lives, but it is the same God who does the work in and through all of us who are his. The Holy Spirit displays God's power through each of us as a means of helping the entire church. (TLB)

2. The diagram on the previous page points out that the Holy Spirit resides in the person. At salvation He joins himself in complete union with the spirit of man (Ro. 8:9-16).

   a. The Holy Spirit's desire is to work outward through all that a person is to bring that special portion of God's love and grace through the individual to other people. Because of the wide diversity in people, their gifts and personalities, God works differently through each individual.

   b. The Holy Spirit chooses to flow supernaturally as He desires through the faculties that each individual yields to Him (1 Cor. 12:11). If there is a need for supernatural ministry on any given occasion, the Spirit of God will use the yielded individual to minister His power in that particular situation.

3. Resident within the Holy Spirit who lives within the believer are all the merciful desires and motivations of Jesus Christ as well as His supernatural powers. Based upon the personality and abilities of the individual, the Holy Spirit chooses to use each one predominately in one of seven different ways: prophecy, serving, teaching, exhortation, organization, giving, or mercy.

   a. The sum of these motivational gifts represent the full desire of Jesus Christ. He was the fullness of God and all of these motivations and desires dwelt in Him simultaneously (Col. 2:9).

LESSON FIVE · UNDERSTANDING SPIRITUAL GIFTS

III. DIFFERENT GIFTS, MINISTRIES, AND WORKINGS

Such is not the case with His followers. Christ has chosen to distribute these motivations separately to individuals. Some are motivated to serve while others desire to teach. This means a teacher in ministering to the needs of others will always be motivated to do things as a teacher would do them.

b. A future lesson will illustrate that as each person functions according to their motivational gift flowing together in unity under the leadership of Christ and His Church, Christ's desire to meet the specific needs of individuals in His body will be fulfilled. Many of Christ's desires are not being fulfilled through His children because many believers are not fully surrendered to His desire to work through them by means of their motivational gift.

4. The Holy Spirit works through every facet of a person's unique make-up. God treats His children individually because no two people are the same in terms of talents, education, creativity, training, experience, personality, and so forth.

a. God's workings are influenced by our personality. The personality (all that a person is, how he thinks, and so forth) must be yielded totally to the Lord. The Holy Spirit then is able to use the uniqueness of each individual to minister Christ's life and love through them. For example, in the natural, Peter's personality agreed with fishing; he loved it. God did not change Peter's love for fishing when He gave him a spiritual calling. He simply made him a fisher of men. God will place the committed individual, one who truly knows himself, in a ministry where he is comfortable and feels most capable.

b. God's workings are influenced by your talents, training, and ability. For example, God chose to use Paul to write twelve books of the New Testament and Peter to write only two. Moses

IV. MINISTERING GOD'S GRACE

2 Peter 3:14-16
So then, dear friends, since you are looking forward to this, make every effort to be found spotless, blameless and at peace with him. [15] Bear in mind that our Lord's patience means salvation, just as our dear brother Paul also wrote you with the wisdom that God gave him. [16] He writes the same way in all his letters, speaking in them of these matters. His letters contain some things that are hard to understand, which ignorant and unstable people distort, as they do the other Scriptures, to their own destruction.

wrote the first five books of the Bible whereas Amos only wrote one. In both cases, God inspired men to write His message while drawing upon the resources of the committed individual. Both Moses and Paul had highly trained and disciplined minds. When those minds finally reached a place of surrender and renewal, God used them to write material that the minds of Peter and Amos were not capable of writing. Peter even admits that Paul wrote things that are difficult to understand (2 Pet. 3:14-16).

5. Diagram Summary

Spiritual gifts work through human personality. The supernatural gifts like the word of wisdom, for example, may draw upon the many facets of our personality: our background, concepts, knowledge, and memory. The Spirit works through our motivational gift, our total personality, and through our physical body as well. In other words, spiritual gifts work through the totality of the yielded individual.

IV. MINISTERING GOD'S GRACE

A. First Peter 4:10

> Each one should use whatever gift he has received to serve others, faithfully administering God's grace in its various forms.

B. God's Free Gift

1. God has a free gift for mankind. That gift is the blessings of His kingdom. He has willed that each one share in the inheritance of His Son. Christ shared the blessings of the kingdom with people while He was here on earth and now He expects His body to do the same thing.

2. People do not deserve God's love and care but He chooses to give it anyway. Each individual is to give away that portion of God's grace that flows through him. It may be an undeserved gift of love and service;

V. MATURITY INCREASES EFFECTIVENESS

an undeserved gift of healing; an undeserved gift of mercy, such as feeding the hungry; or an undeserved gift of caring. All come from the grace of God.

3. The merciful have something to give. The total resources of God's eternal kingdom are at their disposal. The body of Christ and the individual members of that body are givers of the undeserved, unearned gifts of God's kingdom. This is why they minister the grace of God. The Christian, in effect, is an agent of some aspect of God's grace. He is a minister of the vast, unmerited, unearned gift of total and eternal restoration for mankind.

V. MATURITY INCREASES EFFECTIVENESS

A. Maturity: An On-Going Work

God is constantly working to equip the individual in preparation for effective ministry. The individual's effectiveness in ministry and the outworking of God's gifts within him are both subject to his Christian maturity. As we continue to grow in Christ, we become more and more effective since the exercise of our gifts is subject to our maturity in Christ. We may have tremendous gifts, but if we are immature, they will produce little lasting fruit.

B. Equipping Through Experience

1. God's equipping includes the various paths into which He leads each committed disciple. Each disciple's path in life and accompanying set of experiences are as varied as people are in looks and personality. "The steps of a good man are ordered by the Lord" (Ps. 37:23, KJV). Along the way, God will develop His capacity for mercy and compassion. He also will implant a greater understanding of His ways. His desire is to fully equip the disciple, making him or her into a true agent of His mercy and grace.

2. For example, the ministry of some people may be counseling. Perhaps this is because these people

Pathway of Discipleship

LESSON FIVE · UNDERSTANDING SPIRITUAL GIFTS

VI. OVERVIEW

Romans 8:28
And we know that in all things God works for the good of those who love him, who have been called according to his purpose.

2 Corinthians 1:3-7
Praise be to the God and Father of our Lord Jesus Christ, the Father of compassion and the God of all comfort, ⁴ who comforts us in all our troubles, so that we can comfort those in any trouble with the comfort we ourselves have received from God. ⁵ For just as the sufferings of Christ flow over into our lives, so also through Christ our comfort overflows. ⁶ If we are distressed, it is for your comfort and salvation; if we are comforted, it is for your comfort, which produces in you patient endurance of the same sufferings we suffer. ⁷ And our hope for you is firm, because we know that just as you share in our sufferings, so also you share in our comfort.

have themselves faced struggles and have found healing and help in the midst of those struggles. God will use all things, every pain as well as every victory, to minister through them to others (Ro. 8:28). The grace one receives from God can, in effect, be passed on to someone else. This is undoubtedly the meaning of Paul's statement in 2 Corinthians 1:3-7.

3. Not only experience but also personality has its effect on our ministry involvement. Certain personalities will be given to certain aspects of ministry more than others because of who they are in God. Hence, some are anointed to preach, some to do the work of an apostle, some to be hospitable, some to evangelize, and so forth. (Refer in your Home Study Guide to your personal list of spiritual gifts mentioned in the New Testament, Lesson 4, Day 2, questions 1 and 2).

VI. OVERVIEW

1. Each person is equipped with his or her own *charisma* from God. These gifts work through the total individual to minister the grace and mercy of God to others.

2. The total individual is:

   a. Who you are as a person (what you were born with).
   b. Your background and experiences in life.
   c. Your biblical training.
   d. Your secular training.
   e. Your unique gifts, abilities, talents, and so forth.

3. God is working with all committed disciples. He is equipping them for a greater ministry within the framework of who they are. The more fully an individual is equipped, the more effectively God's gifts will be expressed to the world through that individual.

4. Know Yourself

   a. Some are involved presently in areas of service that, for the most part, are outside their areas of giftedness. God wants each believer to discover who they are as a person. Then He will anoint and bless their uniqueness so that they can become an individual expression of His grace to the body of Christ and to the world.

   b. It is essential in our modern culture, which causes men to strive for position, that all believers discover who they are in God. Believers should analyze their unique abilities, small or great, and live up to the fullest of their potential in God. If this is not done, the believer will likely fall into the trap of blindly striving for higher positions in the body of Christ which may not correspond to his personality or gifts.

   c. Romans 12:3-8 confirms what has been stated above.

   Verse 3: "For by the grace given me I say to every one of you: Do not think of yourself more highly than you ought, but rather think of yourself with sober judgment, in accordance with the measure of faith God has given you."

   Comment: In other words, know who you are as a person. Learn what you excel in, what your potential is, and what your limitations are. We must strike a balance between over-rating ourselves and falling into the sin of pride, and under-rating ourselves to the point where we believe we can do nothing for the Lord and that's exactly what we end up accomplishing.

   Verses 4-8: "Just as each of us has one body with many members, and these members do not all have the same function, so in Christ we who are many form one body, and each member belongs to all the others. We have different gifts,

LESSON FIVE · UNDERSTANDING SPIRITUAL GIFTS

according to the grace given us. If a man's gift is prophesying, let him use it in proportion to his faith. If it is serving, let him serve; if it is teaching, let him teach; if it is encouraging, let him encourage; if it is contributing to the needs of others, let him give generously; if it is leadership, let him govern diligently; if it is showing mercy, let him do it cheerfully.''

Comment: In essence, these verses are telling us to discover our potential and then be the very best we can in God.

d. God gives all the faith necessary to facilitate the expression of His gifts through the individual (Ro. 12:3).

VII. SUMMATION

1. God has given every believer a specific portion of His grace in the form of a spiritual gift.

2. Spiritual gifts can be viewed as belonging to one of three categories. There are five supportive-leadership gifts, seven motivational gifts, and nine supernatural gifts.

3. All spiritual gifts are put to use more effectively as the believer matures in Christ. Growth in discipleship is essential to the full and fruitful use of your spiritual gifts.

4. The application of spiritual gifts to the infinite variety of needs in the Church and the world gives rise to a huge variety of ministries or specific expressions of Christian service.

5. The Holy Spirit within the believer works through all that he or she is in terms of personality, education, intelligence, experience, and so forth. This means that the Holy Spirit's workings will never be exactly the same through any two individuals because no two people are exactly alike.

VII. SUMMATION

6. The dangers of jealousy, strife, and division in the body of Christ that arise from our culture's strong competitive urge can be avoided when believers discover who they are in God and begin to function in accordance with their gifts and personality.

home study guide

LESSON FIVE · DAY ONE

SECTION I

1. Study each of the following verses and briefly note what each has to say about the grace of God and what it does for and to the believer.

   a. Jn. 1:14-17 _____

   _____

   b. Ro. 3:21-24 _____

   _____

   c. Ro. 11:1-6 (v. 6) _____

   _____

   d. Ro. 12:6 _____

   _____

   e. 1 Cor. 3:9-10 _____

   _____

   f. 1 Cor. 15:10 _____

   _____

   g. 2 Cor. 8:1-4 _____

   _____

   h. Gal. 2:21 _____

   _____

   i. 2 Tim. 2:1 _____

   _____

2. What is a spiritual gift? _____

   _____

   _____

3. What would you say to a believer who feels he cannot get involved in ministry because he does not possess any spiritual gifts?

   _____

   _____

   _____

   _____

   _____

   _____

103

home study guide

LESSON FIVE · DAY TWO

SECTION II

1. Briefly distinguish between the three types of gifts mentioned in this lesson.

   _____

   _____

   _____

2. a. Why at times do many needs go unmet within the body of Christ?

   _____

   _____

   _____

   b. Have you observed this to be the case at any particular time? Briefly describe one example.

   _____

   _____

   _____

3. Why is it essential for every member of Christ's body to discover, develop, and put to use his spiritual gifts if the world is going to see the fullness of Christ through the Church?

   _____

   _____

   _____

4. Explain the relationship between spiritual gifts and spiritual maturity.

   _____

   _____

   _____

5. List in part (a) those gifts which allow the Church to carry on the supernatural aspect of the earth ministry of Jesus Christ. List in part (b) those gifts which are closely associated with the individual's personality and temperament.

   a. _____   _____

   _____   _____

   _____   _____

   b. _____   _____

   _____   _____

   _____   _____

103

home study guide

LESSON FIVE · DAY THREE

SECTION III

1. What is the difference between a gift and a ministry?

2. List some of the avenues of ministry in your own local church.

3. What ministries do you desire to see added in your church?

4. What part does growth in spiritual maturity play in the development of new ministries in the local church?

5. If someone has a God-given desire to reach out and launch a new avenue of ministry, what should he do first?

home study guide

LESSON FIVE · DAY THREE

SECTION III

6. Use the following diagram from *Pathway 101* to explain what steps a pastor should take to form a new avenue of ministry in the local church.

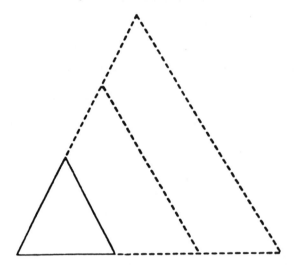

Church leadership base and its expansion

_____

_____

_____

_____

7. Explain what is happening in the following diagram. (Reread *Pathway 101*, Lesson 3, if necessary.)

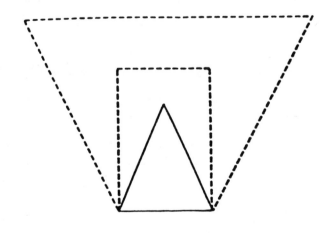

_____

_____

_____

_____

home study guide

LESSON FIVE · DAY FOUR

SECTION III

1. Read the Parable of the Talents in Matthew 25:14-25.

   a. Why were the first and second servants given identical rewards when the first earned 250 percent more money than the second?

   _____

   _____

   b. Can you suggest a reason why all three men were not given the same amount of money to manage?

   _____

   _____

   c. What do your answers in (a) and (b) suggest to you about God's concept of our responsibility with regard to using our spiritual gifts?

   _____

   _____

   _____

   _____

2. "Because all believers are indwelt by the same Spirit, when each one is flowing in accordance with the perfect will of the Spirit, there will be complete uniformity in the way each person ministers God's grace to others." Give reasons why you agree or disagree with this statement.

   _____

   _____

   _____

   _____

3. Give an example from your own experience or that of another Christian of how God uses an individual's background, experience, training, and personality when that individual becomes involved in ministry.

   _____

   _____

4. In what way can it be said that even the supernatural manifestations of the Holy Spirit, such as the word of wisdom or prophecy, are related to the abilities and training of the individual whom the Spirit uses in such a manifestation?

   _____

   _____

   _____

   _____

103

home study guide

LESSON FIVE - DAY FIVE

SECTIONS IV - VI

1. a. According to 1 Peter 4:10, how should we serve others?

_____

_____

   b. What are we ministering to them no matter what form our service takes?

_____

_____

   c. What do your answers to (a) and (b) tell you about the type of attitude we should have as we minister to others?

_____

_____

_____

2. In what sense can God's grace be passed on to someone else? Ro. 8:28; 2 Cor. 1:4-7

_____

_____

_____

_____

3. Briefly relate a personal example of how God used adversity in your life to bless someone else either immediately, or at some later time.

_____

_____

_____

_____

_____

4. How could a proper personal application of Romans 12:3 preserve the local church from the problem of competition and strife over who will hold various positions of ministry such as choir director, organist, or board member for example?

_____

_____

_____

_____

LESSON SIX · THE SUPPORTIVE LEADERSHIP GIFTS

OUTLINE

Lesson Six Update

Lesson Six Synopsis

I. THE SUPPORTIVE GIFTS IN CHRIST'S BODY
A. Ephesians 4:11

II. THE GIFT OF APOSTLESHIP
A. The Human Analogy
B. The Twelve Apostles
C. The Church Today
D. The Apostolic Gift Today

III. THE PROPHETIC GIFT
A. The Human Analogy
B. Old Testament Prophets
C. New Testament Prophets
D. The Prophetic Gift Today

IV. THE EVANGELIST
A. The Human Analogy
B. The Evangelist in the New Testament
C. The Evangelistic Gift Today

V. THE PASTOR-TEACHER
A. The Human Analogy
B. The Pastor-Teacher's Gift Today

VI. THE TEACHER

VII. THEIR COMBINED TASK

VIII. SUMMATION

Home Study Guide

LESSON SIX - THE SUPPORTIVE LEADESHIP GIFTS

LESSON SIX UPDATE

Lesson One   God wants us to share His merciful attitude and imitate His merciful actions toward our fallen world.

Lesson Two   Jesus Christ is the fulfillment of God's mercy. He brings life back to the human family. His eventual work in the world to come will be to restore man totally.

Lesson Three   Jesus prepared the Twelve to continue His ministry of proclaiming and demonstrating the kingdom. He commanded the Church to do the same and then empowered her with the Holy Spirit on the Day of Pentecost.

Lesson Four   The work of Christ continues on earth. His church is literally His hands, His feet, His mouth, His body on earth. To His church He has given His life and authority. Today His body, the Church, is fully equipped and supernaturally endowed to carry on in a multiplied fashion all He came to announce and to peform.

Lesson Five   Christ expresses Himself through the various gifts He has given to each believer. Some have a place of leadership such as pastoring (Eph. 4:11). All have a motivational gift that prompts the submitted individual to fulfill some aspects of Christ's work. All have the Holy Spirit who chooses at His discretion to use the individual in various supernatural expressions of Christ's ministry to the needs of people.

LESSON SIX - THE SUPPORTIVE LEADERSHIP GIFTS

LESSON SIX SYNOPSIS

In this lesson we will study the supportive or leadership gifts in the body of Christ discussed in Ephesians 4:11. Just as the skeletal and muscular systems, the nervous system, the digestive system, and the circulatory system support the human body, these leadership gifts act as the basic life-support systems of the body of Christ.[1]

The apostolic or missionary gift enables some to blaze new trails and lay the basic foundational structure upon which other men build.

The prophetic gift enables some to draw attention to certain things in God's Word and to speak forth what God wants to emphasize to His people.

Those with the evangelistic gift bring the message of God's Word and are successful in leading people to the point of receiving divine life through Christ.

Finally, those with the pastoral gift constantly nourish the body, making sure that it stays in good health. They also help eliminate the wasteful things that would eventually poison the body if allowed to stay. The teacher assists the pastor in this task.

---

[1] Ray C. Stedman, *Body Life* (G/L Regal Books, 1972), pp. 68-79.

LESSON SIX · THE SUPPORTIVE LEADERSHIP GIFTS

I. THE SUPPORTIVE GIFTS

Ephesians 4:11
It was he who gave some to be apostles, some to be prophets, some to be evangelists, and some to be pastors and teachers.

I. THE SUPPORTIVE GIFTS IN CHRIST'S BODY

A. Ephesians 4:11

In Ephesians 4:11, we are told that there are four supportive gifts in the body of Christ.

1. By supportive gifts we mean those gifts that are foundational and absolutely essential to building up and maintaining the body of Christ.

2. The analogy here is taken from the human body. Within the human body there are four major systems upon which the entire body depends in order to function: the skeletal and muscular framework; the nervous system; the digestive system; and the circulatory system.

3. In a most remarkable way the support systems of the human body correspond to the four support ministries in the body of Christ.

4. The four support ministries are apostles, prophets, evangelists, and pastor-teachers (Eph. 4:11). Like the support systems in the human body, these gifts are so essential, that without them, the body of Christ would cease to function.

II. THE GIFT OF APOSTLESHIP

A. The Human Analogy

The gift of apostleship finds its analogy in the skeletal and muscular framework of the human body. Without this framework, the body would be like jelly, unable to stand up or support itself. The apostle's work is foundational. He forms the basic structure that others build upon.

B. The Twelve Apostles

1. The twelve apostles (plus Paul) form the basic structure upon which the rest of the Church is to build until Christ comes. These men laid the basic foundations for the entire Church of Jesus Christ. Ephesians

LESSON SIX · THE SUPPORTIVE LEADERSHIP GIFTS

II. THE GIFT OF APOSTLESHIP

Ephesians 2:19-20
Consequently, you are no longer foreigners and aliens, but fellow citizens with God's people and members of God's household, 20built on the foundation of the apostles and prophets, with Christ Jesus himself as the chief cornerstone.

Hebrews 1:1-3
In the past God spoke to our forefathers through the prophets at many times and in various ways, 2but in these last days he has spoken to us by his Son, whom he appointed heir of all things, and through whom he made the universe. 3The Son is the radiance of God's glory and the exact representation of his being, sustaining all things by his powerful word. After he had provided purification for sins, he sat down at the right hand of the Majesty in heaven.

John 15:26-27
"When the Counselor comes, whom I will send to you from the Father, the Spirit of truth who goes out from the Father, he will testify about me; 27but you also must testify, for you have been with me from the beginning."

Ephesians 2:19-20
Consequently, you are no longer foreigners and aliens, but fellow citizens with God's people and members of God's household, 20built on the foundation of the apostles and prophets, with Christ Jesus himself as the chief cornerstone.

Acts 2:42-47
They devoted themselves to the apostles' teaching and to the fellowship, to the breaking of bread and to prayer. 43Everyone was filled with awe, and many wonders and miraculous signs were done by the apostles. 44All the believers were together and had everything in common. 45Selling their possessions and goods, they gave to anyone as he had need. 46Every day they continued to meet together in the temple courts. They broke bread in their homes and ate together with glad and sincere hearts, 47praising God and enjoying the favor of all the people. And the Lord added to their number daily those who were being saved.

2:19-20 says the Church is built on the foundation of the apostles and prophets with Jesus Christ as the chief cornerstone.

2. These men, flowing with the Holy Spirit, took the principles they had learned from Jesus Christ and began to build the New Testament Church. It is important to understand that the apostles used as their guidelines:

a. The teachings of the Old Testament prophets (Heb. 1:1-3; Acts 8:30-35, 26:19-23).

b. The teachings of Jesus Christ as He had instructed them for three or more years (Jn. 15:26-27).

Since Christ Himself came as a fulfillment of Old Testament prophecy, the Church is built upon the combined truth of the old covenant as well as the new.

3. To Paul was given the task of founding the Church among the Gentiles, or non-Jewish nations. He built as well upon the teachings of Christ and the prophets. He points out that the Church is built upon the ministry of the New Testament prophets as well as those of the Old Testament (Eph. 2:19-20, 3:4-5).

C. The Church Today

1. The modern church is called to build upon the foundational principles laid down for the Church in all ages by the apostles in the New Testament.

2. Throughout the New Testament we discover principles that are adaptable to any age and any culture. For example, Acts 2:42-47 shows us two basic principles which were used effectively by the early church in order to instruct and nurture the believers.

a. The larger group.

They met collectively in the Temple to hear the apostle's instruction, as well as to worship (Acts 2:42-47).

LESSON SIX - THE SUPPORTIVE LEADERSHIP GIFTS

II. THE GIFT OF APOSTLESHIP

Acts 5:42
Day after day, in the temple courts and from house to house, they never stopped teaching and proclaiming the good news that Jesus is the Christ.

b. The small group.

They met from house to house, or in small groups for fellowship over food (Acts 2:46), for teaching (Acts 5:42, 20:20), and for prayer (Acts 12:12).

3. Each church today must take these New Testament principles and apply them to its own individual historical, social, and cultural situation. When a church does this, it will be building, in fact, upon the solid foundation of Christ and His apostles. Such a church will become increasingly biblical in its outlook and will be phenomenally successful.

D. The Apostolic Gift Today

1. In a secondary sense the apostolic gift is still being given today. God still calls men to blaze a new trail and form a basic structure upon which others can build. These are men sent by God to establish a new body of believers in an unreached area.

2. Men with this gift must build the structure according to the principles of Scripture as laid down by the original apostles. There are no new truths or principles that can be added to those of the New Testament. Individuals with this gift take the truth of the written Word and impart it to new churches and ministries that God wants to bring forth in a given time and place.

3. The word "apostle" is synonymous with the word "missionary." The apostolic gift today, therefore, represents the person who goes into virgin territory and:

a. Evangelizes.

b. Gathers a group together and begins to teach them.

c. Guides and nurtures that embryonic work until eldership, deacons, and pastoral gifts are established.

Acts 19:8-10

Paul entered the synagogue and spoke boldly there for three months, arguing persuasively about the kingdom of God. ⁹But some of them became obstinate; they refused to believe and publicly maligned the Way. So Paul left them. He took the disciples with him and had discussions daily in the lecture hall of Tyrannus. ¹⁰This went on for two years, so that all the Jews and Greeks who lived in the province of Asia heard the word of the Lord.

Acts 20:17-20

From Miletus, Paul sent to Ephesus for the elders of the church. ¹⁸When they arrived, he said to them: "You know how I lived the whole time I was with you, from the first day I came into the province of Asia. ¹⁹I served the Lord with great humility and with tears, although I was severely tested by the plots of the Jews. ²⁰You know that I have not hesitated to preach anything that would be helpful to you but have taught you publicly and from house to house.

Acts 20:27

For I have not hesitated to proclaim to you the whole will of God.

Acts 20:28

Keep watch over yourselves and all the flock of which the Holy Spirit has made you overseers. Be shepherds of the church of God, which he bought with his own blood.

d. Moves on to new unevangelized areas.

4. Paul is an excellent example of this ministry. He went to Ephesus, to Corinth, and to many other centers where:

a. He evangelized (Acts 19:8-10).

b. He lived with his converts for an extended period of time (Acts 20:17-20).

c. He taught them, declaring the whole counsel of God to them (Acts 20:27).

d. He stayed with them until elders emerged from within the local body (Acts 20:28).

5. The work of an apostle then is that of a true missionary on the home front as well as the foreign field. God has called mature, tested men to go in to evangelize, start new churches, and see them established, and then move somewhere else.

6. The apostolic gift should be reemphasized in our approach at home and abroad. Local churches and denominations should support proven, seasoned men who are clearly called to evangelize and pioneer new churches. It is not advisable to consider young men just out of Bible school or seminary for such important and difficult apostolic work.

7. In conclusion, the one called to missionary or apostolic work is a person who is a spiritual jack-of-all-trades. He evangelizes; speaks as a prophet, pointing out God's direction for that particular assembly; teaches; and shepherds the flock. All preachers, however, do not have such a gift, just as all preachers are not evangelists.

III. THE PROPHETIC GIFT

A. The Human Analogy

1. The prophetic gift finds its analogy in the nervous system of the human body. The nervous system

LESSON SIX · THE SUPPORTIVE LEADERSHIP GIFTS

III. THE PROPHETIC GIFT

stimulates the body to action. It is connected to the brain and faithfully carries messages to every muscle and organ of the body.

2. There are men and women in the body of Christ who function in much the same way, stimulating the Church to action. They deliver a message which calls the Church to return to the written Word. They clearly articulate that portion of the written Word which Christ, the Head, wants to emphasize to His body. They stimulate the local body, the denominational body, or at times, even the world-wide body of Christ to action.

B. Old Testament Prophets

1. In the Old Testament, God called certain men, such as Samuel, Isaiah, and Amos to be prophets to His people Israel as well as to certain other nations. They became His spokesmen. They delivered and declared God's Word.

2. In the Old Testament we have a permanent record of God's truth given through these prophets (Heb. 1:1).

3. Jesus, since He was the fullness of God, possessed all the gifts including the gift of prophecy. He was the Word of God incarnate. He delivered the Father's message of truth, the fullest and most complete revelation mankind will receive this side of eternity.

C. The New Testament Prophets

1. Prophets are mentioned several times in the New Testament (Acts 11:27, 13:1, 15:32; Eph. 2:20, 3:5).

2. These were men who forcefully preached to believers and exhorted them in accordance with the truths of the new covenant based upon the teaching of Jesus and the apostles.

D. The Prophetic Gift Today

1. A key to understanding the prophetic ministry in the Church today is to view this ministry as distinct

Acts 13:1
In the church at Antioch there were prophets and teachers: Barnabas, Simeon called Niger, Lucius of Cyrene, Manaen (who had been brought up with Herod the tetrarch) and Saul.

III. THE PROPHETIC GIFT

Hebrews 1:1-2
In the past God spoke to our forefathers through the prophets at many times and in various ways, ²but in these last days he has spoken to us by his Son, whom he appointed heir of all things, and through whom he made the universe.

Ephesians 6:17
Take the helmet of salvation and the sword of the Spirit, which is the word of God.

from that of the Old Testament prophets. If this is not done, it will lead to gross misunderstanding and error. The record of what these Old Testament prophets have said is found in the Bible. According to Hebrews 1:1-2, there is no new inspired revelation. God has spoken. The Bible is not still being written. It is complete and final. There is no genuine prophet today speaking anything new or apart from the written record of the Bible.

2. It is important, however, that we view the on-going prophetic gift as God placing emphasis upon a particular part of the written Word. God's written word, the Bible can be viewed as a general epistle, or letter of absolute truth being sent to the world and God's people:

> And we also thank God continually because, when you received the word of God, which you heard from us, you accepted it not as the word of men, but as it actually is, the word of God, which is at work in you who believe.
> (1 Thes. 2:13)

The prophetic ministry speaks forth God's quickened Word (Eph. 6:17). God has something to emphasize for the hour to His people. The emphasis, however, must be drawn from His authoritative revelation of truth, the Bible.

3. There should be a distinction made between the prophetic gift and the gift of the teacher. A teacher is able to take God's Word, dissect it verse by verse and make the depth of what it says known to the people. Here the word of wisdom (deep insight) is in operation: "For to one is given by the Spirit the word of wisdom; to another the word of knowledge by the same Spirit" (1 Cor. 12:8, KJV). The prophetic ministry, however, emphasizes a specific truth from God's Word that God wants His people to respond to on a specific occasion. In other words, God wants them to hear something from the Bible which is particularly applicable to their situation.

4. The prophet is not so interested in deep insight into biblical truth as simply and directly delivering God's clear word or message for the hour.

LESSON SIX - THE SUPPORTIVE LEADERSHIP GIFTS

IV. THE EVANGELIST

5. Every pastor-teacher from time to time is used prophetically. God has something to say to the people he pastors. Some, depending on their gift, are used this way more regularly than others.

6. There are certain men and women in the body who are not so much teachers as they are exhorters. They speak to people's emotions, calling them to respond to the emphasized truth of God's Word that they preach.

IV. THE EVANGELIST

A. The Human Analogy

1. The evangelistic gift finds its analogy in the digestive system of the human body. The digestive system takes food and transforms it into living flesh. The digestive system makes what one takes into the body become life and part of the body. The evangelist leads men to the point where the Spirit can transform them. He has a unique ability to impart to men and women the message of eternal life and actually see them yield to the transformation of God's spirit.

2. All Christians are to witness, but all do not have the gift of the evangelist. This person is called to a special leadership position involving reaching men and women for Jesus Christ.

B. The Evangelist in the New Testament

1. In the New Testament, although all believers shared their faith with others, certain individuals were used by God in an unusual way to bring others into the kingdom.

2. The word *evangelist* simply means one who brings the gospel to others. He proclaims the good news of salvation through faith in Christ.

3. In the New Testament, although Philip the deacon is the only person actually called an evangelist, Paul tells us that Christ has given evangelists to His

Pathway of Discipleship

LESSON SIX · THE SUPPORTIVE LEADERSHIP GIFTS

V. THE PASTOR-TEACHER

Acts 21:8
Leaving the next day, we reached Caesarea and stayed at the house of Philip the evangelist, one of the Seven.

2 Timothy 4:5
But you, keep your head in all situations, endure hardship, do the work of an evangelist, discharge all the duties of your ministry.

Acts 4:4
But many who heard the message believed, and the number of men grew to about five thousand.

Church and He charges Timothy, a pastor-teacher, to do the work of an evangelist (Acts 21:8; 2 Tim. 4:5).

4. The apostle Peter is the outstanding New Testament example of an evangelist. In his first two sermons he won 5,000 people to Christ, not counting the women and children (Acts 4:4).

C. The Evangelistic Gift Today

1. Like Peter and Philip, there are those called to preach the gospel over and over. Their preaching results in men responding to salvation through Jesus Christ (Acts 2:4-25).

2. The evangelist quite often has a personality to blend with his call. Peter is a good example. He was outgoing, spontaneous, forceful, a man of great faith, and undoubtedly, a man of action.

3. Evangelists can truthfully be called God's salesmen. Quite often the similarities are evident. Evangelists have the ability as do salesmen to close the sale, to draw in the net, so to speak, and get a positive response from the listener. All of this, of course, must not be by coercion or human ingenuity. If the results are to be lasting, the Holy Spirit must be the one working through such personalities, empowering them to do the work of evangelism.

4. Evangelists should be underwritten by local churches or the general body of Christ to carry on their work. Evangelists who are part of local assemblies should not only be sent out to proclaim the gospel, but should also equip and instruct others in the local church in how to share their faith effectively.

V. THE PASTOR-TEACHER

A. The Human Analogy

The pastor-teacher's gift finds its analogy in the circulatory system of the human body. The blood carries food and oxygen to every part of the body. It also

LESSON SIX · THE SUPPORTIVE LEADERSHIP GIFTS

V. THE PASTOR-TEACHER

1 Timothy 1:3
As I urged you when I went into Macedonia, stay there in Ephesus so that you may command certain men not to teach false doctrines any longer.

takes away the accumulated wastes. The pastor is one who takes care of the continual feeding, preserving, and cleansing of the local church. He constantly nourishes the life and vitality of the saints of God. He also listens to problems and counsels people until the problems that could be harmful to the body are eliminated. Evangelists deal with spiritual birth in the same way that an obstetrician deals with physical birth. The pastor, however, is like a pediatrician, concerning himself with the growth and development of new infants in the faith. He is also like the general practitioner who deals with good diet and health and the healing of diseases in the body.

B. The Pastor-Teacher's Gift Today

1. Timothy was a bishop or pastor called to carry on the work Paul (an apostle) had founded (1 Tim. 1:3). A pastor builds upon the missionary's foundation.

2. His main functions are to:

   a. Shepherd, i.e., protect and care for the flock. He is assisted in this responsibility by the deacons and deaconesses (Acts 20:28).

   b. Teach and instruct the people in the Word of God (1 Tim. 4:13).

3. Some pastors seem to have additional gifts. Some are particularly effective in evangelism. Such pastor-teachers are often called to a church for a period of time to help equip that body of believers to evangelize more effectively.

4. Some pastors are given more to prophetic preaching rather than to teaching. They impart a clear sense of purpose and vision to the local assembly and exhort God's people to make a positive response to that vision.

5. Every pastor, however, regardless of his own tendencies, must see that his people are properly taught

VI. THE TEACHER

Ephesians 4:11
It was he who gave some to be apostles, some to be prophets, some to be evangelists, and some to be pastors and teachers.

Acts 13:1
In the church at Antioch there were prophets and teachers: Barnabas, Simeon called Niger, Lucius of Cyrene, Manaen (who had been brought up with Herod the tetrarch) and Saul.

1 Corinthians 12:28
And in the church God has appointed first of all apostles, second prophets, third teachers, then workers of miracles, also those having gifts of healing, those able to help others, those with gifts of administration, and those speaking in different kinds of tongues.

through effective methods and anointed instruction, whether it is by him or someone else in the assembly. The point is, he is a pastor-teacher, and should be given to teaching people. There is no other way discipleship can be developed in the local church.

VI. THE TEACHER

A. The Greek of Ephesians 4:11 indicates that the pastor-teacher represents really only one gift. In other words, the teaching gift is a part of the pastoral gift. Every pastor must also be a teacher.

B. In the New Testament, however, there is an indication that some teachers functioned apart from the pastoral ministry. They were itinerant teachers in the body of Christ (Acts 13:1; 1 Cor. 12:28).

C. Today there are also teachers who itinerate (e.g., conference and seminar speakers) or who teach in other settings apart from the pastorate (e.g., Bible colleges, seminaries, Christian writers, and so forth).

D. Such teachers are assistants to the pastor of every church they visit. They come to complement, enhance, and assist the teaching responsibility of the pastor. Even though they travel from church to church, they are strongly tied to the pastoral gift and cannot effectively function without it. Teachers who are not also pastors are primarily called by God to assist the pastor in his ministry of equipping the saints.

VII. THEIR COMBINED TASK

A. God uses these four supportive gifts to build up and equip the saints to be effective as the body of Jesus Christ on earth.

1. Apostles found or establish the basic structure.

2. Prophets emphasize what God is saying to His people on a specific occasion.

3. Evangelists preach the gospel and teach others how to present it effectively.

4. Pastor-teachers oversee the local body feeding and protecting it and moving it toward maturity in Christ.

VIII. SUMMATION

1. The supportive leadership gifts mentioned in Ephesians 4:11 serve the same functions in the spiriutal body that the four major systems do in the human body: the skeletal and muscular framework corresponds to the apostolic gift; the nervous system corresponds to the prophetic gift; the digestive system corresponds to the gift of the evangelist; and the circulatory system corresponds to the gift of the pastor-teacher.

2. The apostle is the one who lays the foundation for the Church. Historically, we look to the twelve apostles and Paul as examples. Today our examples include pioneer missionaries at home and abroad.

3. The prophet today is one who articulates God's specific concerns for the hour to His people. Historically the ministry of the biblical prophets is ours through the pages of the Old and New Testaments.

4. The evangelist is called specifically to a ministry of bringing people to Christ in significant numbers.

5. The pastor is responsible for leading, protecting, and feeding the local church. He does this primarily by teaching the Word of God and is assisted in this work by the teacher.

103

home study guide

LESSON SIX · DAY ONE

SECTION I

1. Why are the four ministries listed in Ephesians 4:11 called supportive leadership gifts?

_____
_____
_____
_____
_____
_____
_____

2. Carefully study Ephesians 4:12-16 and list the reasons why these four support gifts have been given to the Church. What are they to accomplish within the body of Christ?

_____
_____
_____
_____
_____
_____
_____
_____
_____
_____
_____
_____
_____
_____
_____
_____
_____
_____
_____

103

home study guide

LESSON SIX · DAY TWO

SECTION II

1. What other apostles are mentioned in the New Testament besides the Twelve and Paul? Acts 14:14; Ro. 16:7; Gal. 1:19; 1 Thes. 2:7 with Acts 17:1-4

_____

_____

_____

_____

2. What was the distinctive place of importance given to the twelve apostles? Jn 14:26, 15:26-27; Acts 1:13-22; Eph. 2:19-20, 3:4-6

_____

_____

_____

_____

_____

_____

3. In what sense is the apostolic gift in the Church today different from the work of the Twelve plus Paul?

_____

_____

_____

_____

4. Explain why every apostle is a missionary but not every missionary is necessarily an apostle.

_____

_____

_____

_____

5. a. What type of man should a church or denomination look for to pioneer a new church?

_____

_____

_____

b. Who is usually given this task today?

_____

_____

home study guide

LESSON SIX · DAY THREE

SECTION III

1. Using the following references, describe the nature of the prophetic ministry in the Old Testament. Jer. 1:1-10; Eze. 2:1-7

_____

_____

_____

_____

_____

2. What ministry did prophets perform in the New Testament church? Acts 11:27, 13:1-3, 15:32; Eph. 2:20, 3:5; 1 Cor. 14:3-5; Jas. 5:10

_____

_____

_____

_____

_____

_____

3. In what key respect is the ministry of prophets in the Church today different from the ministry of the Old Testament prophets? Heb. 1:1-2

_____

_____

_____

_____

_____

4. What limitations are all prophets subject to? Deut. 13:1-5; Mt. 7:15-20

_____

_____

_____

_____

_____

home study guide

LESSON SIX · DAY FOUR

SECTION IV

1. In what sense can every believer be called an evangelist?

_____

_____

_____

2. What ministry does the evangelist have to perform on behalf of those who are already converted?

_____

_____

_____

_____

3. Explain why, in the case of the evangelist, it is often easy to see how God gives the individual a ministry that is in line with his personality and natural inclinations.

_____

_____

_____

_____

_____

4. Study Acts 8:5-40 and note as many characteristics of an evangelist and his ministry that you can find in the life of Philip the evangelist (Acts 21:8).

_____

_____

_____

_____

_____

_____

_____

_____

_____

_____

_____

_____

home study guide

LESSON SIX · DAY FIVE

SECTIONS V · VI

1. Read Acts 20:28-35 and list all that it says about the ministry of the pastor-teacher, what that ministry is, and how the pastor-teacher is to perform it.

_____
_____
_____
_____
_____
_____
_____
_____

2. In what crucial sense does a local church's organizational structure and the degree of ministry involvement by every member affect the pastor's teaching ministry? Acts 6:1-7

_____
_____
_____
_____

3. a. What does 2 Timothy 2:2 say to you about how your pastor should be spending a significant amount of his time?

_____
_____
_____
_____

   b. Is your pastor able to do this? Why or why not?

_____
_____
_____

4. If an individual has a teaching ministry apart from pastoring, how does his ministry relate to that of the pastor-teacher?

_____
_____
_____
_____
_____
_____
_____

LESSON SEVEN - MOTIVATIONAL GIFTS   Part I

OUTLINE

Lesson Seven Update

Lesson Seven Synopsis

I. INTRODUCTION
A. Premise
B. Other Viewpoints
C. Biblical Evidence
D. Purpose of This Study

II. THE MOTIVATIONAL GIFT APPROACH
A. What Is a Motivational Gift?
B. Distinguishing Between Types of Gifts
C. How Motivational Gifts Function

III. COMMENTARY ON ROMANS 12:1-8
A. The Context
B. Verses 1-2
C. Verses 3-5
D. Verses 6-8

IV. MOTIVATIONAL GIFTS IN ACTION
A. Strengths and Weaknesses
B. Diagram
C. Diagram Explanation

V. SUMMATION

Home Study Guide

LESSON SEVEN - MOTIVATIONAL GIFTS   Part I

LESSON SEVEN UPDATE

Lesson One   God's will is to make His children as merciful in character as He is. He wants them to view the world and feel for the world as He does.

Lesson Two   Jesus was God's mercy taking action, bring life, and, eventually, total restoration to fallen humanity.

Lesson Three   Beginning with Himself, then the apostles, then through His entire Church which He has empowered by the Holy Spirit, Christ seeks to bring forth His kingdom among men.

Lesson Four   The Church is Christ's body. It continues, in an even greater dimension, the work which He began while He was here on earth.

Lesson Five   Christ is expressed through the life of each believer as he commits himself and allows Christ's life flow to others through the exercise of his spiritual gifts.

Lesson Six   The basic life-support structure of the body of Christ is formed by four ministries in the Church: apostles, prophets, evangelists, and pastor-teachers. These gifts hold the body together and are analogous to the body's skeletal and muscular systems, the nervous system, the digestive system, and the circulatory system.

This lesson investigates the second category of gifts mentioned in Scripture. They are often referred to as motivational gifts and are listed in Romans 12:6-8. These gifts show how God motivates individuals to function in a variety of ways within the body of Jesus Christ. God takes the basic personality traits with which we are endowed and calls us to function accordingly within various ministries in the church.

In these last lessons of *Pathway 103*, we focus on some of the practical implications of becoming God's mercy to the world. We encourage you to begin to analyze your unique self in relation to others and find your most suitable place of ministry in the body of Christ.

Pathway of Discipleship

I. INTRODUCTION

Romans 12:3-8

For by the grace given me I say to every one of you: Do not think of yourself more highly than you ought, but rather think of yourself with sober judgment, in accordance with the measure of faith God has given you. ⁴Just as each of us has one body with many members, and these members do not all have the same function, ⁵so in Christ we who are many form one body, and each member belongs to all the others. ⁶We have different gifts, according to the grace given us. If a man's gift is prophesying, let him use it in proportion to his faith. ⁷If it is serving, let him serve; if it is teaching, let him teach; ⁸if it is encouraging, let him encourage; if it is contributing to the needs of others, let him give generously; if it is leadership, let him govern diligently; if it is showing mercy, let him do it cheerfully.

1 Peter 4:10

Each one should use whatever gift he has received to serve others, faithfully administering God's grace in its various forms.

I. INTRODUCTION

A. Premise

1. There are strong indications in Romans chapter 12 verses 3-8 that God gives to each person a predominant motivational gift. This motivational gift dictates how each person eventually seeks to function in the body of Christ.

   a. Romans 12:3 indicates that every person should know their place in the body of Christ:

   Do not think of yourself more highly than you ought, but rather think of yourself with sober judgment, in accordance with the measure of faith God has given you.

   After stating this fact, Paul lists seven gifts or ways that people express themselves through the body of Christ.

   b. The seven gifts listed in verses 6-8 show some of the various ways members of Christ's body are motivated to function.

   c. 1 Peter 4:10 says that each person has received a primary or predominant gift from God. Peter goes on to state that each person should employ their primary gift to serve others.

B. Other Viewpoints

Not all Bible scholars agree that these are motivational gifts. A popular alternative viewpoint is that the gifts mentioned in Romans 12:6-8 are simply a smattering of many gifts in the body of Christ. In this view, Paul is simply urging Christians to discover their gifts and anointed abilities.

C. Biblical Evidence

Careful scrutiny of each of the three major texts that deal with spiritual gifts lends considerable support to the concept of motivational gifts.

Pathway of Discipleship

LESSON SEVEN · MOTIVATIONAL GIFTS **Part I**

I. INTRODUCTION

1 Corinthians 12:1-11
Now about spiritual gifts, brothers, I do not want you to be ignorant. [2] You know that when you were pagans, somehow or other you were influenced and led astray to dumb idols. [3] Therefore I tell you that no one who is speaking by the Spirit of God says, "Jesus be cursed," and no one can say, "Jesus is Lord," except by the Holy Spirit.
[4] There are different kinds of gifts, but the same Spirit. [5] There are different kinds of service, but the same Lord. [6] There are different kinds of working, but the same God works all of them in all men.
[7] Now to each one the manifestation of the Spirit is given for the common good. [8] To one there is given through the Spirit the message of wisdom, to another the message of knowledge by means of the same Spirit, [9] to another faith by the same Spirit, to another gifts of healing by that one Spirit, [10] to another miraculous powers, to another prophecy, to another the ability to distinguish between spirits, to another the ability to speak in different kinds of tongues, and to still another the interpretation of tongues. [11] All these are the work of one and the same Spirit, and he gives them to each one, just as he determines.

Ephesians 4:11-12
It was he who gave some to be apostles, some to be prophets, some to be evangelists, and some to be pastors and teachers, [12] to prepare God's people for works of service, so that the body of Christ may be built up.

Romans 12:3-8
For by the grace given me I say to every one of you: Do not think of yourself more highly than you ought, but rather think of yourself with sober judgment, in accordance with the measure of faith God has given you. [4] Just as each of us has one body with many members, and these members do not all have the same function, [5] so in Christ we who are many form one body, and each member belongs to all the others. [6] We have different gifts, according to the grace given us. If a man's gift is prophesying, let him use it in proportion to his faith. [7] If it is serving, let him serve; if it is teaching, let him teach; [8] if it is encouraging, let him encourage; if it is contributing to the needs of others, let him give generously; if it is leadership, let him govern diligently; if it is showing mercy, let him do it cheerfully.

1. In 1 Corinthians 12:1-11, it is evident from the context (i.e., chapter 14) that Paul is writing about the spontaneous, supernatural expressions of the Holy Spirit.

   a. These take place spontaneously through various members of the body of Christ especially during times of collective worship.

   b. In 1 Corinthians chapter 12, verse 1, Paul uses the Greek word *pneumatikon* which is usually translated, "spiritual gifts." Concerning this word, one scholar has written,

   > The use of pneumatikos (of which *pneumatikon* is a form) in the epistles of Paul always bears the connotation, "supernatural." The gifts of the Spirit are not natural talents. They are supernatural manifestations of the Holy Spirit.[1]

2. In Ephesians chapter 4, verse 11, it is evident that Paul is refering to a different type or category of gifts. Here the emphasis is not upon the supernatural, spontaneous expression of the Holy Spirit, but upon the gifts of leadership that support and equip the Church.

   a. In Ephesians chapter 4, the expression of the gift is not momentary such as would be the case for the word of wisdom or a gift of healing. These gifts are of a more permanent nature refering to the life-long ministry of an individual. God gives individuals to be apostles, prophets, evangelists, or pastor-teachers, commissioning them to continually equip the saints for the work of the ministry.

   b. In Ephesians 4 it is evident that these individuals are gifts to the entire church given to equip the saints for the work of the ministry. They are not simply individual supernatural manifestations that are given through various individuals to meet a particular need at a moment in time.

3. When we come to Romans chapter 12, verses 3-8, the key word seems to be "function."

[1] Howard M. Ervin, *These Are Not Drunken As Ye Suppose* (Logos International, 1968) p. 233. For a full study of the use of the word *pneumatikos* in Paul's epistles see pages 227-233.

Pathway of Discipleship

I. INTRODUCTION

a. The Greek word used is *praxis*. It literally means a person's ongoing business or function in the body of Christ. The connotation is that of a deed which is incomplete and in progress. The term, therefore, seems to speak of our ongoing work or function in the body of Christ.

b. In verses 4 and 5, Paul compares the body of Christ with the human body pointing out that even though there is unity in the body, there is also diversity of function. Each member has his own different approach to ministry based upon the particular motivational gift each has received.

c. Verse 6 says, "We have different gifts, according to the grace given us." The Holy Spirit graciously gives to each individual believer a gift that motivates them to function in a particular fashion in the body of Christ.

4. In summary,

a. The gifts mentioned in 1 Corinthians chapter 12, emphasize how the Holy Spirit spontaneously ministers with supernatural manifestations through various members in the body of Christ.

b. The gifts in Ephesians chapter 4, verse 11, emphasize God's calling upon certain individuals for the special work of giving life support to the body and equipping the saints for the work of the ministry.

c. Finally, the gifts now under study mentioned in Romans chapter 12, verses 6-8, emphasize how the various members in the body of Christ tend to function or approach their ministry in the body of Christ.

D. **Purpose of This Study**

Studying these gifts in Romans chapter 12 as basic motivations of the Spirit in the believer's life can prove helpful in some of the following ways:

I. INTRODUCTION

1. Such a study helps us to understand how the body of Christ functions.

   a. In order to meet every need in the body of Christ and the world, Christ motivates committed individuals to express themselves predominantly in one of seven areas.

   b. When Christ was here, He had all the motivational gifts working through Him. Therefore, He was all things to all men. Now, however, He distributes these gifts among the members of His body.

   c. The church, which is His body on earth today with its variously gifted members, now becomes all things to all men.

2. A study of motivational gifts helps us discover our own predominant characteristics. This helps to direct us into appropriate areas of ministry.

3. This study can help us understand and appreciate others who think differently than we do. We can begin to see the reason why others approach the work of God as they do and why they are motivated to do the things they do.

4. a. Whatever our gift may be, Paul instructs us in essence to apply the measure of faith God gives to help us function. Christ desires the gift to have its fullest expression through our personalities and abilities. God has given to every man a measure of faith to function uniquely for Him.

   b. If we do not know who we are, and what our predominant gift is, then it is doubtful that we can effectively exercise the measure of faith which the Holy Spirit has given to us to fulfill our ministry.

   c. Quite clearly, some people are functioning in areas where they do not belong because they have not discovered who they are in Jesus Christ. An understanding of motivational gifts could remedy this situation.

II. THE MOTIVATIONAL GIFT APPROACH

5. An understanding of motivational gifts can be extremely helpful to the local church in the task of placing individuals into ministry.

   a. When new areas of ministry are opened up, or boards or committees are formed for various purposes, how much more effective would it be if those with the appropriate motivational gift were selected.

   b. A church can greatly benefit by understanding motivational gifts when in the process of selecting pastoral staff. The church with a multiple pastoral staff should fill needed positions with people who have a predominant motivational gift that corresponds to the area of ministry responsibility they will occupy.

II. THE MOTIVATIONAL GIFT APPROACH

A. What Is a Motivational Gift?

1. When a person comes to Christ, God chooses to motivate them in certain ways. God knows the predominate characteristics of each person and sets them apart to be used according to how He has made them. To be effectively used of God, a person should discover their predominant motivation in life.

2. A motivational gift relates to how God chooses to use an individual in any one of numerous avenues of ministry. It describes the predominant tendency or way in which that individual will approach anything that they undertake for the Lord.

3. a. Like the supernatural expressions of the Spirit, a person's motivational gift works through their innate abilities, training, experience, creativity, and so forth. As has already been stated in Lesson 5, the workings of God are different in every individual's life. Two people may have the same motivational gift but be entirely different as to their avenues of ministry.

II. THE MOTIVATIONAL GIFT APPROACH

b. For example, one person may work in a bus ministry while another works in the church office. Although these two ministries are different, if both individuals possess the motivational gift of service, they will function in their respective ministries in much the same way. Their main thrust will be to serve the tangible needs of others.

4. Therefore, every believer should discover his predominant motivational gift and then find a place of ministry in the local body that corresponds to his abilities, training, inclination, and personality.

B. **Distinguishing Between Types of Gifts**

Although we have already mentioned the distinction the Scripture makes between the types of gifts in Ephesians 4, 1 Corinthians 12, and Romans 12, we must begin to understand this in a very practical way.

1. For example, a person may have the support gift of pastor-teacher in the body but have the motivational gift of exhortation. Such an individual will be motivated to build up (exhort or encourage) others constantly through his role of teaching in the body.

2. A person may have a motivational gift of teaching, but not hold the position of a full-time pastor-teacher. They will always, however, approach their ministry analytically and pay close attention to detail.

3. The person who has the motivational gift of prophecy (intuitive understanding, Ro. 12:6) will not necessarily be chosen of the Spirit to be used supernaturally in the gift of prophetic utterance (1 Cor. 12:10). One has to do with how the individual intuitively approaches any area of ministry. The other is the Holy Spirit emphasizing God's truth to the body on a given occasion for a specific purpose or need. By the same token, this individual with a motivational gift of prophecy does not necessarily possess the support gift of prophet in the body of Christ (Eph. 4:11).

II. THE MOTIVATIONAL GIFT APPROACH

C. How Motivational Gifts Function

1. Jesus had all seven of these motivational gifts operative in His life. The Church, which is His body on earth, also has all seven of these gifts functioning. These seven gifts are distributed among the various individual members of the body.

2. a. One motivational gift predominantly flows through each individual. A person is happy and comfortable once they are functioning in accordance with their primary gift. It is their essential mode of operation in the body of Christ. This is not to say that they do not possess many of the characteristics seen in the other six motivational gifts, but one of these gifts seems to be more predominant than the others.

   b. Research seems to indicate that in many cases, individuals can identify a primary as well as a secondary motivational gift. This secondary gift, although not as strong as the primary one, does take precedence over other ways of functioning. It must be remembered that the categories of Romans 12 should not be defined too rigidly.

   c. Understanding our predominant motivation is further complicated by the fact that our motivational gift expresses itself through the complexity of our personality and training.

3. It is important to note that all believers are called upon to function to some extent in all of the seven areas regardless of their predominant tendency. We should know our predominant gift, but in no way should it excuse us from fulfilling other essential obligations set forth in Scripture. For example, the Bible exhorts every Christian to serve others (Gal. 5:13), to teach one another (Col. 3:16), to exhort or encourage one another (Heb. 3:13), and to be merciful (Lk. 6:36).

4. All seven gifts mentioned are needed to keep Christ's body in balance. Competition is eliminated and all

Galatians 5:13
You, my brothers, were called to be free. But do not use your freedom to indulge the sinful nature; rather, serve one another in love.

Colossians 3:16
Let the word of Christ dwell in you richly as you teach and admonish one another with all wisdom, and as you sing psalms, hymns and spiritual songs with gratitude in your hearts to God.

Hebrews 3:13
But encourage one another daily, as long as it is called Today, so that none of you may be hardened by sin's deceitfulness.

Luke 6:36
Be merciful, just as your Father is merciful.

Pathway of Discipleship

III. COMMENTARY ON ROMANS 12:1-8

needs are met as each member understands where they fit and how they are contributing to the growth of the body as a whole.

III. COMMENTARY ON ROMANS 12:1-8

It is very important that we understand the context of the Scripture where these motivational gifts are listed. For this reason, we present the following brief commentary on Romans 12:1-8.

A. The Context

1. In the first eleven chapters of Romans, Paul has presented a treatise on the doctrine of salvation. He has demonstrated the sinfulness of all men and their universal guilt before God. He has shown how men are justified through faith and can be delivered from not only the penalty, but also the power of sin through Christ. To Paul, this was the only gospel and the only way to salvation for both Jew and Gentile.

2. The Christian life, however, is more than knowing correct doctrine. Practical application of doctrine must be made to every area of life. For this reason, in most of Paul's epistles, the preliminary chapters deal with doctrine while those which follow make practical application of that doctrine to everyday Christian living. Such is the case with the Book of Romans. For this reason, Romans 12:1 begins "Therefore. . . ." This is the turning point at which the doctrinal treatise now focuses upon the practical truths of Christian living. Since God has provided all that is necessary for salvation and deliverance from sin, believers are called to live in a certain manner which Paul begins to set forth.

B. Verses 1-2

1. "I urge you, brothers, in view of God's mercy,"

Salvation came because of God's love and mercy for

III. COMMENTARY ON ROMANS 12:1-8

His creation. We chose to love Him and serve Him because He first loved us.

2. "To offer your bodies as living sacrifices,"

Here the apostle is saying on the basis of all that God has done for you, and as a result of His mercy, present your bodies to Him. Our body is the temple of the Holy Spirit and the instrument through which He works. We are, therefore, to yield our members to all that the Holy Spirit wants to do in and through us. In the next four chapters of the Book of Romans, Paul describes the practical implications of this sacrifice. What he sets forth is a life-style similar to that described by Jesus in the Sermon on the Mount. Presenting ourselves to God as living sacrifices will involve everything from submission to authority to honoring the needs of a weaker brother in order to maintain Christian unity.

3. "Holy and pleasing to God—"

Following the precepts presented in chapters 12-15 will produce a life that is holy and pleasing to God.

4. "Which is your spiritual worship,"

Worship is not something that simply takes place at a public meeting. All of life becomes spiritual worship when it is given over to the renewing process of the Holy Spirit. This results in a life that outwardly exemplifies the character of Jesus Christ.

5. Verse 2

"Do not conform any longer to the pattern of this world, but be transformed by the renewing of your mind" (v. 2a).

None of the things mentioned in chapters 12-15 are possible until first the Christian surrenders his mind to the renewing and sanctifying process of God's Word and the Holy Spirit. What Paul describes as

III. COMMENTARY ON ROMANS 12:1-8

the Christian life-style is the result of a change in our thinking. As our philosophy becomes oriented toward God's kingdom, then our behavior does as well. There can be no shortcuts to holy living. It is not a work of the flesh or of human thinking or ability. It must flow from a mind renewed and cleansed by the Word of God.

6. "Then you will be able to test and approve what God's will is—his good, pleasing and perfect will" (v. 2b).

    a. The first thing in Paul's mind regarding the will of God is the importance of knowing our place and function in the body of Christ. This he describes in verses 3-8. If we continue to be worldly, we are going to pollute our gift and cancel its value by selfish and sinful living. As we allow the Holy Spirit to renew our minds through the Word of God, it becomes clearer and clearer what our function and ministry is. It is something we grow into.

    b. Generally speaking, our culture and our educational system do not train us well in knowing who we really are. We are taught to be competitive and to strive for position. We are brought up in a materialistic society that says we have to have certain things. Often, we begin to serve Jesus Christ not knowing who we really are.

    c. Knowing who we are does not necessarily come instantaneously. It comes about as we allow the renewing work of purity to take place in our minds. As the Word of God begins to purify us, and we choose no longer to conform to the philosophy of this world, we begin to understand more clearly our function in the body of Christ. This is why our study in *Pathway of Discipleship* up to this point has been so important. It is only through spiritual development and growth in discipleship that we really come to a deep understanding of our function in the body. Once we have come to that understanding based upon

III. COMMENTARY ON ROMANS 12:1-8

our motivational gift or gifts, then we are able to test and approve through experience God's good, pleasing, and perfect will.

C. Verses 3-5

1. "For by the grace given me I say to every one of you: Do not think of yourself more highly than you ought, but rather think of yourself with sober judgment (v. 3a)."

   a. The renewing process eventually must lead to a proper estimate of yourself. This includes an honest assessment of your abilities, talents, and spiritual gifts. This is needed so desperately because our culture tends to push people beyond their own potential and often places them where they do not belong. In business, for example, this is called the Peter Principle. An individual reaches his area of highest competence and then, because of a competitive desire to strive ahead, is promoted to the next level beyond his competence where he is unable to rise any further. This results in individuals being left in positions where they do not belong simply because of competitive striving for so-called higher positions regardless of their true gifts.

   b. Self-knowledge is also the path of true humility because it protects us from the dangers of both self-conceit and false modesty. Self-knowledge brings forth an approach to Christian service void of the competition and striving that is so much a part of the world system. Many in the body of Christ have not made this discovery as yet and so they are frustrated in trying to serve the Lord. We can never reach our fullest potential in serving God until this process of self-discovery takes place. Coming to a full understanding of who we are in Christ in one sense, is the same as coming to an understanding of God's will for our lives. Such a statement assumes that we understand the distinction between the sinful nature or flesh as Paul calls it and the true, new self

III. COMMENTARY ON ROMANS 12:1-8

which is "being renewed in knowledge in the image of its creator" (Col. 3:10).

    c. Self-knowledge can also help us find our most effective place of ministry because it frees from arbitrarily choosing our place. It also protects us from guilt motivation by others who urge us to take up areas of service for which we may not be equipped. They do this simply because there is a need for personnel in that area.

2. "In accordance with the measure of faith God has given you" (v. 3b).

God is the one who gives us first of all, the faith to grasp the nature of our spiritual gift. This faith also helps us understand the extent of our talents and abilities. We must never forget the Parable of Talents in Matthew chapter 25. We are not equally endowed or gifted, nor does God give to us equal responsibilities. It is up to us to seek His wisdom and discover our place in His kingdom.

3. "Just as each of us has one body with many members, and these members do not all have the same function, so in Christ we who are many form one body, and each member belongs to all the others" (vv. 4-5).

As has been stated before, the key word is "function." Just like the human body, the various members of the body of Christ have different functions based upon the different gifts they have been given (v. 6, see also Section I, C, 3).

D. Verses 6-8

"We have different gifts, according to the grace given us. If a man's gift is prophesying, let him use it in proportion to his faith. If it is serving, let him serve; if it is teaching, let him teach; if it is encouraging, let him encourage; if it is contributing to the needs of others, let him give generously; if it is leadership, let him govern diligently; if it is showing mercy, let him do it cheerfully."

1. The seven gifts mentioned here will be studied in more detail in the following lesson. With prophecy, however, Paul makes a key point with reference to all the gifts. He says, "If a man's gift is prophecying, let him use it in proportion to his faith." In a sense, this can be applied to all the gifts. We should never get beyond ourselves in our understanding of who we are and thus fall into pride. On the other hand, neither should we underestimate our potential. There is a delicate balance that only the Holy Spirit can reveal to each individual. Most believers, it would seem, do not live up to their total potential in God because their faith in God's ability to use them is limited.

2. Undoubtedly, Paul is also refering here to the many people in the body of Christ who never fully understand their gifts. If they really understood who they were in God, then they would allow their gift to function in its fullest dimension. For example, the pastor who is predominately a server may be constantly intimidated because he comes up short in the area of administration. He could make the mistake of spending much time trying to make up his shortcomings in the area of administration, not realizing that the other members of the body are available to compensate for his weakness in this area.

IV. MOTIVATIONAL GIFTS IN ACTION

A. Strengths and Weaknesses

1. As we will see in the next lesson, each gift has its strengths as well as its weaknesses.

   a. Part of the on-going renewing and sanctifying process of the Holy Spirit is to work on our weaknesses, enabling us to be more effective. Understanding our predominant motivational gift, therefore, can never be used as an excuse for accepting the weaknesses that often accompany a particular gift.

IV. MOTIVATIONAL GIFTS IN ACTION

b. The Holy Spirit seeks constantly to conform us to the image of Jesus Christ who, although He possessed all the gifts, did not possess their accompanying weaknesses. As we focus upon the way in which He exercised each of the gifts, we can discover how to overcome the weaknesses associated with our own particular gifts.

2. Nevertheless, the point should be stressed that it is the other members of the body that compensate most for the areas of our own weakness.

a. An example would be the illustration mentioned in the section above of a pastor who is a server. Undoubtedly, this pastor who is weak in the area of administration can improve through learning how to manage an organization more effectively. Nevertheless, he will never be as good an organizer as the person who has the predominant motivational tendency of administration. Therefore, this pastor must call upon the other members of the body to compensate in the areas where he is weak.

b. Culture suggests to us that we should not admit our weaknesses. Yet the Bible says that because we are members of one another, we should learn to depend upon one another. This suggests that as we begin to understand ourselves, and each other, we can learn how to work interdependantly and thus approach what it means to be the fullness of Christ. The weaknesses of one member are balanced by the gifts of another.

3. Once we come into an understanding of our gifts and the gifts of others, we can avoid the situation that happens so often in the local church:

"The Marthas, busily preparing the church's annual spaghetti supper, complain about the Marys who seem interested only in Bible studies and prayer groups. And the committee on stopping the flood of pornographic material in local stores cannot understand why so few individuals attend the meetings where a protest is being organized. Bill, the men's Bible teacher for as long as

IV. MOTIVATIONAL GIFTS IN ACTION

anyone can remember, delights in giving extensive word studies during his Sunday classes. He wonders why more men do not share his enthusiasm."[2]

And on it goes. These sources of disharmony can only be resolved once we understand who we are and who our fellow believers are in their area of ministry in the body of Christ.

(Section IV continues with the diagram on the next page.)

---

[2] Lawrence F. Selig, *Discover Your Motivational Gifts,* unpublished manuscript.

B. Diagram: Group in Flooded Church Basement Responding to Crisis According to Their Basic Motivational Gifts.[3]

PROPHET: "God has a message in this if we will only listen."

SERVER: "I'll go fix some coffee for you workers."

GIVER: "I would like to start a fund raising drive so the damage can be fixed as soon as possible."

ADMINISTRATOR: "Bob, you get some buckets from the closet. Joe, the mops are in the furnace room. Jim . . . ."

TEACHER: "I recall this same thing happened back in 1948 when Pastor Smith was on vacation. The water was not discovered for 12 hours, and by that time . . . ."

EXHORTER: "There are some good illustrations in spiritual growth which we can all learn from this experience."

MERCY: "Oh, I know how upset the women will be when they learn their Spring Banquet will be postponed!"

[3] Lawrence F. Selig, *The Varieties of Motivations Necessary for Christian Community to Function, A Study of Spiritual Gifts in Romans 12:6-8 and Some Implications for a Local Congregation* (Unpublished doctoral thesis, 1983), pp. 95-96.

IV. MOTIVATIONAL GIFTS IN ACTION

C. Diagram Explanation by Larry Selig[3]

1. "When all seven of the motivations are working and flowing together in harmony, the work of Christ is most completely accomplished. Let me illustrate this with an experience in a former church. One evening, I went to the church social hall located in the basement. For several days, we had experienced severe rainstorms. When I reached the basement, there was water flooding a large section of the floor. Let us assume a large group of members were with me, representing all seven motivational gifts. The following suggests how each one may have responded to this crisis:

   a. "*Prophet* 'God has a message in this if we will listen. The trustees were aware of the leak for months and should have arranged for necessary repairs before more damage was done. We all need to be more diligent in our responsibilities for the Lord.' This motivation comes with a word of correction.

   b. "*Administrator* 'Bob, you get some buckets from the closet. Joe, the mops are in the furnace room. Jim, see if you can go get a ladder from the shed to see if any leaves are plugging the drains on the roof. . . .' This motivation gets the bucket brigade into action, knowing where the resources are to do the job.

   c. "*Teacher* 'I recall this same thing happened back in 1948 when Pastor Smith was on vacation. The water was not discovered for 12 hours, and by that time, the whole floor was ruined. It cost over $500 to have Johnson Flooring do the repairs.' What a mind for facts and details!

   d. "*Exhorter* 'There are some good illustrations in spiritual growth which we can all learn from this experience. Every crisis has a silver lining.' You can be sure this floor will appear in a Sunday School lesson taught by the exhorter on the next Sunday.

---

[3] Lawrence F. Selig, *The Varieties of Motivations Necessary for Christian Community to Function, A Study of Spiritual Gifts in Romans 12:6-8 and Some Implications for a Local Congregation* (Unpublished doctoral thesis, 1983) pp. 95-96.

IV. MOTIVATIONAL GIFTS IN ACTION

e. "*Giver* 'I would like to start a fund drive so the damage can be fixed as soon as possible.' This motivation senses right away that funds will be needed for repairs.

f. "*Mercy* 'Oh, I know how upset the women will be when they learn their Spring Banquet will be postponed.' What empathy for the disappointment some are going to feel.

g. "*Server* 'I'll go fix some coffee for you workers.' God bless those faithful servers. Every church has them. How easily we overlook the many things they do!

"All of these responses are appropriate. None of them alone completely deals with the issue. But when all of them flow together in harmony, the crisis is met and the balanced ministry is achieved."[3]

2. How important it is that we recognize and affirm each other's gifts in the body of Christ. Imagine this same situation of flooding in the church basement and how things would have gone if the individual members, instead of concentrating upon the task at hand and responding in accordance with their gifts, concentrated upon the responses of each other and became critical. We can just imagine the administrator overhearing the teacher as he says, "I recall the same thing happened back in 1948 when Pastor Smith was on vacation. The water was not discovered for twelve hours and by that time. . . ." Administrator: "Who cares what happened in 1948. We've got a problem to fix now!" Or imagine the one with the motivation of giving overhearing the person who has the motivational gift of mercy saying, "Oh, I know how upset the women will be when they learn their Spring Banquet will be postponed." Giver: "Who cares about the Spring Banquet! Do you know what this is going to cost?"

3. In a sense, what was illustrated in the previous paragraph is simply another example of the situation Paul describes in 1 Corinthians chapter 12,

---

[3]Lawrence F. Selig, *The Varieties of Motivations Necessary for Christian Community to Function, A Study of Spiritual Gifts in Romans 12:6-8 and Some Implications for a Local Congregation* (Unpublished doctoral thesis, 1983) pp. 95-96.

verses 12-26. In this passage, Paul seems to say that the believers of Corinth were busy condemning each other's gifts and not recognizing their value to the body:

> The eye cannot say to the hand, "I don't need you!" And the head cannot say to the feet, "I don't need you!" On the contrary, those parts of the body that seemed to be weaker are indispensable, and the parts that we think are less honorable we treat with special honor.
>
> (1 Cor. 12:21-22)

All of the members of the body are essential for its proper functioning. Once we understand our motivational gifts, and those of our fellow believers, we can see the beautiful balance of gifts that Christ has placed within His body and flow together in love and cooperation to accomplish the work of His kingdom.

V. SUMMATION

1. God gives to each person a predominant motivational gift which dictates how they will function in the body of Christ. These are listed in Romans 12:6-8.

2. In 1 Corinthians chapter 12, Paul lists spontaneous supernatural expressions of the Holy Spirit which are given at various times through various members of the body. In Ephesians chapter 4, he deals with gifts that involve life-long vocations of ministry in the body of Christ for the purpose of equipping others.

3. Acquiring an understanding of the concept of motivational gifts can help us to function harmoniously in the body of Christ. It can also help us discover our own gifts and thus find the most fruitful and fulfilling avenues of ministry involvement.

4. A motivational gift relates to how God chooses to use an individual and the predominant way in which they will approach whatever He calls them to do.

5. The possession of any given motivational gift does not restrict areas of potential involvement for the

V. SUMMATION

Lord but only determines the style with which we will approach whatever ministry we become involved in.

6. Christ had all seven motivational gifts operating fully in His life. As the body of Christ learns to flow together in unity and harmony depending upon one another, it becomes the fullness of Christ to the world.

7. It is essential that we come to know who we are in Christ and be aware of our motivational gift. This will help us discover our most effective place of ministry in the body.

8. As we mature in Christ through the process of discipleship, we become more aware of who we are in Christ. This leads us to a knowledge of where He wants us to function in ministry.

103

home study guide

LESSON SEVEN · DAY ONE

SECTIONS I-II

1. Briefly distinguish between the types of gifts described in 1 Corinthians chapter 12, Ephesians chapter 4, and Romans chapter 12.

_____

_____

_____

_____

2. In what way can a study of motivational gifts be helpful to us personally?

_____

_____

_____

_____

_____

3. Explain in your own words the concept of motivational gifts.

_____

_____

_____

_____

_____

4. Have you ever had the experience of being involved in a church board or committee and observing the beautiful variety of motivational gifts operating to fulfill all needs? If so, briefly describe this experience. You may wish to consult the precise gift definitions and lists of weaknesses and strengths found on the chart at the end of the home study for this lesson.

_____

_____

_____

_____

_____

_____

_____

_____

103

home study guide

LESSON SEVEN · DAY TWO

SECTIONS II-IV

1. List specific examples from the ministry of Jesus of the functioning of each of the seven motivational gifts listed in Romans 12:6-8.

   a. Prophecy _____

   b. Serving _____

   c. Teaching _____

   d. Exhortation _____

   e. Giving _____

   f. Administration _____

   g. Mercy _____

2. Have you ever tried to "cop-out" on a particular distasteful area of involvement on the basis of the excuse, "That's not my gift"? Briefly explain the situation.

   _____

   _____

   _____

3. How has your personal growth in discipleship and your experiencing the process of mind renewal spoken of in Romans 12:1-2 helped you to understand yourself and your spiritual gift(s)?

   _____

   _____

   _____

   _____

   _____

4. Can you identify any individuals in your own local church who seem to be so different in their way of serving the Lord? Has this lead to incidences of disharmony in the past? Briefly explain the situation.

   _____

   _____

   _____

   _____

5. How can the study of motivational gifts help us work harmoniously with others in the body of Christ?

   _____

   _____

   _____

154

home study guide

LESSON SEVEN · DAY THREE

Instructions

Your home study for today consists of completing the followng test to help you discover your primary motivational gift.[4]

1. Read through the list of seventy statements and place a check beside the answer which is *most* appropriate for you: "Usually True, Sometimes True, Seldom True, Rarely True." *Do not ponder at length over any one question. Be as realistic as you can, answering not as you would like to be, but as you are at this stage in your life.*
2. After completing the seventy statements, transfer the numerical value of your answers to the Tabulation Chart found on page 5. Then add the scores horizontally in each line and record the total at the right.
3. The total will help reflect your spiritual gift. Your primary motivational gift should be indicated by the largest number of points. One or more other motivational gifts may also rank above the others. These may be considered secondary motivations. Compare these primary and secondary motivations with the definitions on page 163.
4. Once you have completed the test and tallied your score, spend some time answering the questions for personal study or group discussion that follow. These are designed to help you evaluate your present place of ministry in the body of Christ in the light of what you have discovered about your motivational gifts through the test.

Beside each statement check the appropriate box which comes closest to your normal tendency.

	Usually True (5)	Sometimes True (3)	Seldom True (1)	Rarely True (0)
1. I like to think of ways to help others who are suffering physically, emotionally, and spiritually.				
2. I enjoy spending time in intense study and research of the Bible.				
3. I feel people should say what they mean, and mean what they say about God's truth even though it may hurt the feelings of the listeners.				
4. I give more than the biblical tithe to the Lord's work.				
5. I enjoy responsibilities which involve helping other Chrisitans grow spiritually.				
6. I enjoy doing small tasks that need to be done, without being asked to do them.				
7. I like to take a project, break it down into various parts, and systematically organize a plan to accomplish the final goal.				
8. I find it very difficult to discipline others unless I am *really* convinced it will help them.				
9. In studying the Bible, I like to study the passage in context and find what it meant to the writer before trying to apply it to myself.				
10. When situations are not right, I feel an urge to speak up about them in order to correct them.				
11. When I hear of someone in need, I think of the amount of money I can give to help them.				

[4] This test was developed by Rev. Lawrence F. Selig. © 1984 by Christos Publishing Company, Inc. All rights reserved. Reproduction is strictly prohibited. Additional copies are available from Christos Publishing Company, Inc., 1267 Hicks Blvd., Fairfield, OH 45014.

home study guide

LESSON SEVEN · DAY THREE

	Usually True (5)	Sometimes True (3)	Seldom True (1)	Rarely True (0)
12. I am a possibility thinker, believing that all things are possible with God.				
13. I would rather do a task myself than work with a group or committee to get it done.				
14. If a project needs to be done and no one is in charge, I like to volunteer to get it organized.				
15. I can sense immediately whether the person I am talking to is hurting, or is really happy.				
16. I organize my thoughts in a systematic way after careful research and study.				
17. I have the unique ability to discern deception, dishonesty, and compromise in the motives and actions of others.				
18. I prefer to give to the work of the Lord amounts suggested by the Lord rather than have others suggest how much I should give.				
19. I have the ability to help people see how their trials and difficulties can be opportunities for spiritual growth.				
20. I would rather do a number of short-range immediate tasks than do one long-range task task taking a year or more.				
21. I have the ability to see over-all goals and the "finished picture" of a project, when others may see only the various pieces.				
22. I will go to almost any length to avoid hurting the feelings of others.				
23. I like to see things prepared and taught in a systematic, factual way rather than having people share just personal experiences.				
24. Injustice, dishonesty, and unrighteousness in the church and community bother me enough that I am willing to speak up even though some may be offended.				
25. When I feel led by the Lord to give, I give generously without thinking of the sacrifice this may involve.				
26. I would rather talk with someone about their personal problems and share with them practical help from the Bible than send them to someone else.				
27. I find it difficult to say no when I see something practical which can be done to help someone in need.				
28. I would rather train others to do various tasks than do everything myself.				
29. I like to speak kind, comforting, reassuring words to others and I am hurt when I hear others speak harshly.				
30. I enjoy communicating biblical truths to others and seeing long-range growth in knowledge of the Christian faith.				
31. I have a desire to share with others messages I believe are from God which can correct, encourage, and comfort them.				

home study guide

LESSON SEVEN · DAY THREE

	Usually True (5)	Sometimes True (3)	Seldom True (1)	Rarely True (0)
32. I enjoy making my home available for entertaining overnight guests who are involved in God's work.				
33. I enjoy meeting regularly over a period of time with individuals to help them grow spiritually.				
34. I enjoy serving the needs of others in order to free them for more important work for the Lord.				
35. I have the ability to organize people, resources, plans and timetables in order to accomplish the Lord's work efficiently.				
36. When others are hurting or in pain, I can *feel* for them, even to the point of becoming emotionally involved.				
37. I have the ability to explain difficult issues, after giving them much thought and study.				
38. I am able to communicate my thoughts directly and frankly to close friends, even though they may disagree with me.				
39. I think it is sinful if a person fails to manage his/her financial assets well.				
40. I enjoy teaching and sharing with others, especially when I can apply the Bible to daily life.				
41. I enjoy doing routine tasks to help others, even though the tasks seem menial.				
42. I feel comfortable delegating responsibilities to others and directing a plan through to completion.				
43. I am primarily attracted to people who express tenderness and kindness.				
44. I enjoy researching answers to difficult questions.				
45. When I fail to live up to the standards of Christian living which I feel are important, I become very discouraged with myself.				
46. I really enjoy giving money and other material resources to Christian causes.				
47. When sharing Christian truth, I enjoy illustrating it with personal examples to make it more practical.				
48. I need reassurance that what I do to help other people is appreciated.				
49. I am able with discipline to work under pressure and accomplish things, as long as I know my goals and objectives.				
50. I feel deep compassion and understanding for those with spiritual and emotional needs.				
51. The meaning of words and how people use them is important to me.				

103

home study guide

LESSON SEVEN · DAY THREE

	Usually True (5)	Sometimes True (3)	Seldom True (1)	Rarely True (0)
52. I speak up about what I believe is right and wrong, regardless of whether others agree or not.				
53. I receive special joy in encouraging others to be more generous in their giving.				
54. I enjoy sharing the practical teaching of Scripture as it relates to the personal and emotional problems of people.				
55. When I provide things for others, I would rather give them something I made myself than something I bought.				
56. In a leadership position, I feel more joy than frustration or burden.				
57. I like to be involved in alleviating the sufferings of others.				
58. When I hear a message I like, I check out the facts and details if I am uncertain rather than accept the speaker's word without question.				
59. When I sense the problems and needs of the world, I am burdened to spend long periods of time in intercessory prayer.				
60. When I give money or other tangible help to others, I like to do it anonymously.				
61. I like to simplify complex issues into practical steps to help people grow spiritually.				
62. I am a *now* person, and when I see a need, I want to meet it right away rather than wait for a more convenient time.				
63. I enjoy being responsible for the success of the organization or group of which I am a part.				
64. I avoid leadership positions where I will have to carry out decisions which may hurt the feelings of some people.				
65. I enjoy devoting great amounts of time to studying the Bible to learn new truth.				
66. When I share God's truth with others, I need to see that this brings about the change that God desires in them.				
67. I enjoy living at a lower standard of living than necessary in order to have more to give to the Lord's work.				
68. I like to share with others the confidence that in spite of outward circumstances, trials, and set-backs, God always keeps His promises.				
69. When I hear of some practical need that someone has, I am willing to volunteer to help meet it.				
70. I am willing to endure the misunderstanding and reaction of others when working on a plan, because I know the end results of what I am seeking to accomplish.				

home study guide

LESSON SEVEN · DAY THREE

After completing the final question, check back to make sure all questions are answered and then transfer your scores to the Tabulation Chart below.

Tabulation Chart

In the boxes below, enter the numerical value of your responses to questions 1-70, (Usually True - 5, Sometimes True - 3, Seldom True - 1, Rarely True - 0). Then, add up the ten numbers horizontally and record the result in the totals column at the right.

										Totals	
1	8	15	22	29	36	43	50	57	64		Mercy
2	9	16	23	30	37	44	51	58	65		Teaching
3	10	17	24	31	38	45	52	59	66		Prophecy
4	11	18	25	32	39	46	53	60	67		Giving
5	12	19	26	33	40	47	54	61	68		Exhortation
6	13	20	27	34	41	48	55	62	69		Serving
7	14	21	28	35	42	49	56	63	70		Administration

When you meet together with your group next week, be prepared to share your predominant tendency with the other group members as they will do with you so that these can be filled in on the list found on page 162.

home study guide

LESSON SEVEN · DAYS FOUR AND FIVE

The following questions are designed to assist you in evaluating your present place of ministry in the body of Christ particularly in the light of what you have learned through taking the motivational gift test.

1. Having discovered your primary motivational gift, are you presently involved in areas of service for the Lord which enable your strongest motivations to be expressed? Explain your answer.

_____

_____

_____

_____

_____

_____

_____

_____

_____

_____

2. Are the characteristic strengths and weaknesses of your motivational gift reflected in your service for the Lord? Explain your answer. See the chart following the Home Study Guide for this lesson. (Note: For a fuller understanding of the characteristics and strengths of your motivational gift(s), please turn to Lesson 8.)

_____

_____

_____

_____

_____

_____

_____

_____

_____

_____

_____

_____

_____

103

home study guide

LESSON SEVEN · DAYS FOUR AND FIVE

3. Study the list of weaknesses for your particular motivational gift and suggest some ways you could turn these into personal strengths.

_____

_____

_____

_____

_____

_____

_____

4. What additional training could help balance your areas of weakness and develop further areas of strength with regard to your motivational gift?

_____

_____

_____

_____

_____

_____

5. Are you presently allowing others to use their complementary gifts in your area of ministry?

_____

_____

_____

_____

_____

_____

6. What other areas of ministry in your local church are you aware of where your primary gift could perhaps be put to better use?

_____

_____

_____

_____

_____

_____

home study guide

STUDY GROUP GIFT LIST

Below list the primary motivational gift of each of the other members of your study group. Beside each name, note any characteristics of their predominant motivational gift that you have noticed in their behavior or work for the Lord.

1. _____

2. _____

3. _____

4. _____

5. _____

6. _____

7. _____

8. _____

9. _____

10. _____

Motivational Gift Definitions

Gift	Definition	Strengths	Weaknesses
Mercy	The ability to identify with and comfort those in distress.	• A special sensitivity to emotional needs. • Sensitivity for the feelings of people which expresses tenderness, kindness, and compassion. • Generally likes to avoid actions which will hurt the feelings of others, including discipline and administrative decisions.	• May become too emotionally involved and lose objectivity in helping others. • Can become closed in spirit to those who are not sensitive to others. • Tends to avoid stress-producing situations and firmness, unless absolutely convinced it is necessary. • There is a danger of emotional involvement in helping those of the opposite sex.
Teaching	The ability to clarify truth after thorough study and research.	• Likes to present truth in a systematic fashion. • Enjoys the world of books and ideas.	• May become more interested in factual details than the practical application of truth. • May enjoy personal research more than teaching others. • May become proud of their learning and knowledge.
Prophecy	The ability to declare God's truth which touches the heart and brings conviction.	• The gift of "sanctified criticism." • Great ability to verbalize truth and to feel what God feels and see things from God's viewpoint. • Quick to discern dishonest character and motives. • Speaks frankly, even to friends, without considering the consequences.	• May have little sensitivity for the feelings of others. • May appear judgmental. • Is more concerned with righteousness than with people.
Giving	The ability to contribute generously of financial and material resources for the Lord's work.	• Usually desires to give anonymously and at the Lord's prompting. • Usually thrifty and a good financial manager thus has more to give away than others.	• May become cause-oriented rather than people-oriented. • Tends to judge those who are poor financial managers. • Sometimes forgets to confirm giving with spouse.
Exhorting	The ability to encourage others to grow spiritually, even in the face of hardship and suffering.	• Seeks to teach the practical application of Scripture often in a person-to-person setting. • Serves as "God's cheerleader" in the church. • Desires to create harmony in the church.	• May be success-oriented and thus neglect people with deeper, more complex needs. • May tend to oversimplify complex issues.
Serving	The ability to show love by meeting the practical needs of others.	• Ability to recall personal likes and dislikes of others. • Likes to give things made with their own hands. • Enjoys short-range "now" projects. • Volunteers readily ror even menial tasks.	• May disregard personal needs, stamina, family and personal funds in serving others. • Finds it difficult to say no. • May prefer to work alone rather than with others.
Administration	The ability to coordinate people, resources, and schedules to achieve goals.	• Ability to see over-all goals and objectives and the steps needed to reach those goals. • Enjoys seeing all of the parts in the project come together. • Enjoys delegating responsibility and taking leadership when none exists.	• May be task-oriented rather than people-oriented. • Willingness to endure reaction in meeting the goal may appear as insensitivity. • May appear to use people. • May be weak in listening skills.

Lesson Eight Update

Lesson Eight Synopsis

Introduction

I. THE GIFT OF PROPHECY
A. Definition
B. The Greek Term
C. Characteristics
D. Areas for Growth
E. Biblical Examples
F. Christ's Example

II. THE GIFT OF SERVING
A. Definition
B. The Greek Term
C. Characteristics
D. Areas for Growth
E. Biblical Examples
F. Christ's Example

III. THE GIFT OF TEACHING
A. Definition
B. The Greek Term
C. Characteristics
D. Areas for Growth
E. Biblical Example
F. Christ's Example

IV. THE GIFT OF EXHORTATION
A. Definition
B. The Greek Term
C. Characteristics
D. Areas for Growth
E. Biblical Examples
F. Christ's Example

V.   THE GIFT OF GIVING
A. Definition
B. The Greek Term
C. Characteristics
D. Areas for Growth
E. Biblical Examples
F. Christ's Example

VI.   THE GIFT OF ADMINISTRATION
A. Definition
B. The Greek Term
C. Characteristics
D. Areas for Growth
E. Biblical Examples
F. Christ's Example

VII.   THE GIFT OF MERCY
A. Definition
B. The Greek Term
C. Characteristics
D. Areas for Growth
E. Biblical Examples
F. Christ's Example

VIII.   SUMMATION

Home Study Guide

LESSON EIGHT - MOTIVATIONAL GIFTS Part II

LESSON EIGHT UPDATE

Lesson One   Jesus Christ revealed the nature of God's mercy to us so that we could display the mercy of God to the world as we become more and more like Him.

Lesson Two   Christ was God's mercy in action on earth. He brought God's healing, saving life back to man. His life, death, and resurrection made it possible for all who believe to taste God's redemption and restoration in this life, and to experience its fulness in the life to come.

Lesson Three   Jesus proclaimed and demonstrated the kingdom, and then trained twelve men to do the same. He commissioned His Church to multiply and continue this ministry of proclamation and demonstration, and empowered her with the Holy Spirit to accomplish the task.

Lesson Four   The Church is the body of Jesus Christ on earth. It is a group of people called together to be distinct from the world in life-style and philosophy. This group has been sent by Christ to demonstrate the principles of God's kingdom throughout the earth. The Church is literally the physical extension of Jesus Christ into this world. As every believer discovers and develops his spiritual gifts under the leadership of Christ and with the empowering of the Holy Spirit, the Church becomes effective as Christ's body. God wills that every local church fully become everything that Jesus Christ would be to the community if He were there in person.

Lesson Five   In order to fulfill His purpose, Christ gives to each believer one of the motivational gifts mentioned in Romans chapter 12. Also, to some believers in particular, He gives one of the supportive leadership gifts found in Ephesians chapter 4. In addition, each believer, being indwelt by the Holy Spirit, has within him potential to exercise the nine supernatural gifts found in 1 Corinthians chapter 12. These nine gifts equip the church to continue the supernatural aspect of Christ's ministry.

Lesson Six   The supportive leadership gifts in the body, those of the apostle, prophet, evangelist, and pastor-teacher, correspond to the four basic life-support systems of the human body. Their work is essential to keep the body healthy and to equip it to fulfill its God-given task.

Lesson Seven   At conversion, God takes the basic motivational tendency of each individual and makes it a gift. Through these gifts, He seeks to meet every need in the body of Christ and the world. A person's motivational gift does not determine what type of ministry they will undertake. It does, however, indicate the manner in which they will function in ministry. An understanding of motivational gifts can greatly assist believers to live and work together in harmony.

In this lesson, we will examine in detail the seven motivational gifts mentioned in Romans 12:6-8.

We will look at a concise definition for each of these gifts and study the New Testament Greek terms used for each gift. A list of characteristics showing the strengths and weaknesses for each gift will also be provided. In addition, we will examine one or more people in the Bible who possessed each gift.

Finally, we will look at how each gift was manifested in the life of Jesus Christ. Because of His sinless perfection, knowledge of His example will help us overcome the weaknesses associated with our own predominant motivational gift.

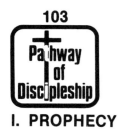
Romans 12:6-8
We have different gifts, according to the grace given us. If a man's gift is prophesying, let him use it in proportion to his faith. [7] If it is serving, let him serve; if it is teaching, let him teach; [8] if it is encouraging, let him encourage; if it is contributing to the needs of others, let him give generously; if it is leadership, let him govern diligently; if it is showing mercy, let him do it cheerfully.

Introduction

In this lesson we will examine the basic characteristics for each of the seven motivational gifts found in Romans 12:6-8. We will set forth a concise definition for each gift and give some insights from the original Greek words used to describe each gift.

In addition, we will look at an example of biblical characters who exhibited the characteristics of each gift.

Finally, we will draw upon the example of the life of Christ who possessed all seven of these gifts without their accompanying weaknesses.

In studying this lesson, we recommend that you pause after reading the section on each gift and complete the questions in the Home Study Guide that pertain to that particular gift. The relevant questions are listed at the end of each section.

Due to the length of this lesson, you might like to begin by studying your own predominate motivational gift based upon the questionnaire you completed at the end of Lesson 7. In addition, as you study each gift, consult the list of the predominant motivational gifts of the other members of your study group also found at the end of the last lesson. As you study the particular characteristics of a gift, keep in mind anyone on your Study Group Gift List who has that gift and see if you can recall observing any of those characteristics in their lives.

I.   THE GIFT OF PROPHECY

The Intuitive Person

A. Definition

1. Those who possess the motivational gift of prophecy have an intuitive ability to size up a given situation from God's perspective.

2. They hold the line on God's standard of truth and righteousness.

3. Their words often touch the heart and bring conviction, causing individuals to right certain wrongs in the body of Christ.

4. Some have called this the motivational gift of insight. The prophetic ability intuitively discerns or understands the inner motivations of people.

5. Because of the identical terms used in English, it is important that we distinguish between the three types of prophetic gifts:

   a. There is the motivational gift of prophecy which describes the predominant way in which an individual will approach their ministry in the body of Christ.

   b. There is the supportive gift of the prophet mentioned in Ephesians 4:11. This is a specific role in the church that assists in equipping the saints for the work of the ministry.

   c. Finally there is the supernatural gift of prophecy. This gift spontaneously emphasizes a particular aspect of God's truth to a particular group of people on a given occasion. This gift is generally associated with the corporate worship service and is mentioned in 1 Corinthians 12:10.

B. The Greek Term

The Greek word for this gift, *prophēteian* means, "speaking forth of the mind and council of God. . . . It is the declaration of that which cannot be known by natural means . . . it is the forth-telling of the will of God, whether with reference to the past, the present, or the future."[1] The prophet has the intuitive ability to sense and the boldness to declare the application of God's truth to the specific situation he is facing.

C. Characteristics

1. Strengths

   a. The prophet has the ability to verbalize truth with little forethought or preparation in the Word.

---

[1] W. E. Vine, *Expository Dictionary of New Testament Words* (Fleming H. Revell Co., 1966) Vol. 3, p. 221.

The purpose of this gift is not so much to inform as with a teacher, but rather, to awaken and motivate people to righteousness.

b. This person has the ability to speak very frankly in declaring the truth. He will do this even to friends, regardless of the consequences.

c. The prophet sees God's coming judgment upon sin unless there is repentance. Because his convictions are so firm, people around him are also convicted of sin.

d. The prophet emphasizes the practical steps that a repentant person must follow in order to stay on the path of righteousness.

e. The prophet has the courage to reprove evil openly regardless of the cost of himself.

f. The prophet sees things from God's viewpoint and feels deeply. He is, therefore, a person of passion and at times, can be overwhelmed with emotion when facing disobedience and injustice. This can facilitate a profound identification with those who are suffering and usually leads to the ministry of intercessory prayer.

g. The prophet has the ability to discern swiftly and accurately the true character of others. He is not deceived by outward appearances or a smooth personality. Hence, the prophet is quick to discover dishonesty of motives as well as compromise.

h. The prophet will accept only righteousness of life as the proof of a person's relationship with God. "Faith without works is dead" is a key concept in his thinking (Jas. 2:26).

i. The prophet frequently appeals to Scripture to support his authoritative declarations. His favorite phrase is, "Thus saith the Lord. . . ."

      j. The propnet has an unusual ability to endure criticism.

2. Weaknesses

      a. The prophet can sometimes intimidate others by his frankness and forcefulness.

      b. With his emphasis on righteousness, the prophet often refuses to compromise and therefore, sometimes appears very rigid.

      c. Because the prophet acts decisively upon his intuitions, and because he does not fear the consequences of his actions and statements, he can appear impulsive to others.

      d. At times the prophet can be very judgmental and and negative in outlook. He faces the danger of becoming overly pessimistic. It is possible, therefore, for this gift to be exercised destructively.

      e. The prophet is not usually a people-person. He is often more concerned with truth and righteousness than with relationships. For this reason, he can appear insensitive to the feelings of others.

      f. The prophet can be subject at times to deep depression and uncertainty.

D. Areas for Growth

1. Because of his insensitivity to the feelings of others, and his strong desire to express himself verbally, the prophet can benefit from training in listening skills.

2. Because of his emphasis on sin and judgment, the prophet needs to heed the exhortation of Romans 12:9:

      a. "Love must be sincere." The prophet is so quick to denouce the sin that he forgets to love the sinner.

I. PROPHECY

Luke 3:19-20
But when John rebuked Herod the tetrarch because of Herodias, his brother's wife, and all the other evil things he had done, ²⁰Herod added this to them all: He locked John up in prison.

Luke 3:10-14
"What should we do then?" the crowd asked.
¹¹John answered, "The man with two tunics should share with him who has none, and the one who has food should do the same."
¹²Tax collectors also came to be baptized. "Teacher," they asked, "what should we do?"
¹³"Don't collect any more than you are required to," he told them.
¹⁴Then some soldiers asked him, "And what should we do?"
He replied, "Don't extort money and don't accuse people falsely—be content with your pay."

Luke 7:18-20
John's disciples told him about all these things. Calling two of them, ¹⁹he sent them to the Lord to ask, "Are you the one who was to come, or should we expect someone else?"
²⁰When the men came to Jesus, they said, "John the Baptist sent us to you to ask, 'Are you the one who was to come, or should we expect someone else?'"

John 18:10
Then Simon Peter, who had a sword, drew it and struck the high priest's servant, cutting off his right ear. (The servant's name was Malchus.)

Mark 8:31-33
He then began to teach them that the Son of Man must suffer many things and be rejected by the elders, chief priests and teachers of the law, and that he must be killed and after three days rise again. ³²He spoke plainly about this, and Peter took him aside and began to rebuke him.
³³But when Jesus turned and looked at his disciples, he rebuked Peter. "Out of my sight, Satan!" he said. "You do not have in mind the things of God, but the things of men."

b. "Hate what is evil; cling to what is good." This exhortation will protect the prophet from becoming overly pessimistic. Although he recognizes the need to identify and cry out against evil, at the same time he must not forget that which should call forth praise.

3. Because of his stern call for judgment and righteousness, the prophetic gift needs to be balanced by the presence of those who have the gift of exhortation (encouragement and upbuilding) and also the gift of mercy (deep sympathy for the needs of others).

E. Biblical Examples

1. John the Baptist provides a prime example of a person with the motivational gift of prophecy (Mt. 3:1-15; Lk. 3:3-20).

   a. John spoke out boldly against sin regardless of the consequences to himself (Lk. 3:19-20).

   b. He knew and proclaimed the practical steps that the repentant person must take to follow the path of righteousness (Lk. 3:10-14).

   c. He experienced a time of depression and uncertainty when thrown into prison (Lk. 7:18-20).

2. The apostle Peter also serves as a secondary example of this gift.

   a. He discerned through the Holy Spirit the wrong motives of Ananias and Sapphira (Acts 5:3-10).

   b. He was impulsive as indicated by his stepping out of the boat to walk on the water. We also see his brash action in defense of the Lord when he cut off the ear of the high priest's slave in the Garden of Gethsemane (Mt. 14:28-31; Jn. 18:10).

   c. Peter was quick to rebuke anything he thought to be out of the will of God including Christ's declaration of His impending death (Mk. 8:31-33).

John 4:16-19
He told her, "Go, call your husband and come back."
¹⁷ "I have no husband," she replied.
Jesus said to her, "You are right when you say you have no husband. ¹⁸ The fact is, you have had five husbands, and the man you now have is not your husband. What you have just said is quite true."
¹⁹ "Sir," the woman said, "I can see that you are a prophet.

Matthew 13:57
And they took offense at him.
But Jesus said to them, "Only in his home town and in his own house is a prophet without honor."

Matthew 21:11
The crowds answered, "This is Jesus, the prophet from Nazareth in Galilee."

3. Other individuals in Scripture with this motivation would include the prophets of the Old Testament, particularly Jeremiah and Amos who showed an unusual ability to endure criticism (Jer. ch. 28; Amos 7:10-17).

F. Christ's Example

1. The Lord Jesus manifested this gift in some of the following ways:

   a. He discerned the situation of the woman at the well (Jn. 4:16-19).

   b. He fearlessly rebuked the Pharisees even though it meant they would eventually plot His death (Mt. 23:13-36).

   c. Jesus mourned deeply over the fate of Jerusalem because of her sins (Mt. 23:37-39).

   d. Jesus spoke of himself as a prophet saying that as such, He did not receive honor in His own country (Mt. 13:57).

   e. Those who heard Christ preach and teach recognized that He was a prophet (Mt. 21:11).

2. As those with the prophetic motivation seek to become more like Christ, they will find the weaknesses associated with this gift being balanced by the other characteristics of Christ as they come forth. For example, although Jesus rebuked sin very directly, He also manifested perfect love. He was able to hate the sin, and yet love the sinner (Lk. 7:44-48).

   Complete Day One, questions 1-3 in the Home Study Guide.

II. THE GIFT OF SERVING

The Action Person

A. Definition

The one with the motivational gift of serving has the ability to show love by meeting the practical needs of others.

B. The Greek Term

1. In the Greek New Testament, the word *diakonian* which is translated "serving" in Romans 12:7, refers to ministry in a number of different forms. It can refer to preaching the gospel and also to the work of aiding others through the distribution of alms or charity. It is also the word used for the office of a deacon and comes originally from a term that meant waiting on tables i.e., serving food.

2. In Romans 12:7, the meaning centers on meeting the material rather than the spiritual needs of others. It can be defined then, as practical assistance in whatever form that assistance should take in a given situation.

C. Characteristics

1. Strengths

   a. The server has a burning desire to meet the practical needs of others and hence volunteers readily even for menial tasks.

   b. The server enjoys short-ranged projects and wants to get the job done as soon as possible.

   c. The server can be very impatient with red tape and wants to meet the need now. As a result, the server may prefer to work alone.

   d. The server has tremendous physical stamina which enables him to spend long hours in his work of service.

   e. The server has the ability to detect and meet needs that go unnoticed by others.

   f. The server is a task-oriented as opposed to a person-oriented individual. He is more concerned with getting the job done than with developing and maintaining good relationships with people.

g. The server enjoys supporting others behind the scenes and freeing them to do their work for the Lord.

h. Servers are very sacrificial people and will go out of their way to meet the needs they perceive, even using their own personal resources.

i. The server has the ability to recall the likes and dislikes of individuals and thus can minister to them on a very personal level.

j. Servers like to give things made with their own hands and hence, if a church banquet is planned by a group of servers, the food will be homemade. If the same banquet were planned by a group of administrators, it would probably be catered.

2. Weaknesses

a. The server finds it hard to say no to any task and as a result, can become too busy and suffer from exhaustion. This tendency also makes this person vulnerable to exploitation in the church.

b. Servers have a tendency to neglect spiritual needs, particularly their own, because they fail to see the value of anything but the task at hand. As a result, things like Bible study, prayer, and worship may seem to be low on their list of priorities.

e. Servers expect everyone else to be like them, and therefore, can appear pushy to others.

d. Servers can be critical of others who do not seem as willing to sacrifice as they are. This can show up particulary within their own family. They expect their family to sacrifice so as to free them to do their work of service to others.

e. Servers can end up undermining relationships because of their narrow focus on the job at hand and their desire to accomplish it as quickly as possible.

f. Servers can easily be frustrated by the scope of the needs they face because they desire to meet them so quickly.

g. Servers need appreciation and recognition to confirm that their service is fulfilling a need. Without this kind of affirmation, they can become very discouraged.

D. Areas for Growth

Paul's two exhortations in Romans 12:10 provide good advice for the server:

1. "Be devoted to one another in brotherly love" is an important exhortation for the server to keep mind. He must understand his tendency to be critical of others who do not share his sacrificial attitude toward the ministry of service.

2. "Honor one another above yourselves" is also a word for servers. They need to recognize and honor those who have gifts differing from their own and appreciate the benefits of the diversity of gifts in the body of Christ.

E. Biblical Examples

1. Martha (Lk. 10:38-42; Jn. 11:17-40, 12:2).

In Martha of Bethany, the sister of Lazarus and Mary, we see many of the characteristics of a server:

a. In Luke 10, we see Martha distracted by all the work involved in preparing a wonderful meal for the Lord. Here we see the concern for short-range goals as well as the desire to get the job done as quickly as possible.

b. We also see in Martha the critical attitude toward those who do not share her gift i.e., she complains to the Lord about her sister, Mary, who preferred to sit down and listen to Jesus as He taught.

Luke 10:38-42
As Jesus and his disciples were on their way, he came to a village where a woman named Martha opened her home to him. ³⁹She had a sister called Mary, who sat at the Lord's feet listening to what he said. ⁴⁰But Martha was distracted by all the preparations that had to be made. She came to him and asked, "Lord, don't you care that my sister has left me to do the work by myself? Tell her to help me!" ⁴¹"Martha, Martha," the Lord answered, "you are worried and upset about many things, ⁴²but only one thing is needed. Mary has chosen what is better, and it will not be taken away from her."

John 12:2
Here a dinner was given in Jesus' honor. Martha served, while Lazarus was among those reclining at the table with him.

John 13:1-17

It was just before the Passover Feast. Jesus knew that the time had come for him to leave this world and go to the Father. Having loved his own who were in the world, he now showed them the full extent of his love.

² The evening meal was being served, and the devil had already prompted Judas Iscariot, son of Simon, to betray Jesus. ³ Jesus knew that the Father had put all things under his power, and that he had come from God and was returning to God; ⁴ so he got up from the meal, took off his outer clothing, and wrapped a towel around his waist. ⁵ After that, he poured water into a basin and began to wash his disciples' feet, drying them with the towel that was wrapped around him.

⁶ He came to Simon Peter, who said to him, "Lord, are you going to wash my feet?"

⁷ Jesus replied, "You do not realize now what I am doing, but later you will understand."

⁸ "No," said Peter, "you shall never wash my feet."

Jesus answered, "Unless I wash you, you have no part with me."

⁹ "Then, Lord," Simon Peter replied, "not just my feet but my hands and my head as well!"

¹⁰ Jesus answered, "A person who has had a bath needs only to wash his feet; his whole body is clean. And you are clean, though not every one of you." ¹¹ For he knew who was going to betray him, and that was why he said not every one was clean.

¹² When he had finished washing their feet, he put on his clothes and returned to his place. "Do you understand what I have done for you?" he asked them. ¹³ "You call me 'Teacher' and 'Lord,' and rightly so, for that is what I am. ¹⁴ Now that I, your Lord and Teacher, have washed your feet, you also should wash one another's feet. ¹⁵ I have set you an example that you should do as I have done for you. ¹⁶ I tell you the truth, no servant is greater than his master, nor is a messenger greater than the one who sent him. ¹⁷ Now that you know these things, you will be blessed if you do them.

c. In Christ's answer to Martha's complaint, we see the need for the server to not neglect spiritual concerns. He said, "You are worried and upset about many things, but only one thing is needed. Mary has chosen what is better, and it will not be taken away from her" (Lk. 10:41-42).

2. John Mark, who had gone with Paul and Barnabus on their first missionary journey, is also an example of one with a gift of serving. Paul wrote to Timothy concerning Mark and said, "Bring him with thee: for he is profitable to me for the ministry (the *diakonian*, the same word used in Romans 12:7) (2 Tim. 4:11, KJV).

F. Christ's Example

1. The Lord Jesus manifested the motivational gift of service in the following ways:

a. Jesus said of Himself, "The Son of Man did not come to be served, but to serve, and to give his life as a ransom for many" (Mt. 20:28).

b. In Philippians 2, we read that Christ began His work of service the moment he entered upon the Incarnation. He "did not consider equality with God something to be grasped, but made himself nothing, taking the very nature of a servant" (Phil. 2:6-7).

c. We see the practical manifestation of the gift of serving in the life of Christ when He stooped to wash the feet of His own disciples (Jn. 13:1-17).

d. Jesus was constantly concerned for the practical needs of others. In Mark chapter 8, we read,

During those days another large crowd gathered. Since they had nothing to eat, Jesus called his disciples to him and said, "I have compassion for these people; they have already been with me three days and have nothing to eat. If I send them home hungry, they will collapse on the way, because some of them have come a long distance."

(Mk. 8:1-3)

John 19:26-27
When Jesus saw his mother there, and the disciple whom he loved standing nearby, he said to his mother, "Dear woman, here is your son," ²⁷ and to the disciple, "Here is your mother." From that time on, this disciple took her into his home.

Jesus then proceeded to feed four thousand people miraculously because of His concern for their practical needs.

2. In taking Jesus Christ as our perfect example, those with the motivational gift of serving should see the balance He maintained in His life-style.

   a. He served people, yet did not neglect their spiritual needs.

   b. He took the necessary steps to sustain Himself. He avoided the crowds at times, not allowing Himself to be pushed to the point of exhaustion through the continual work of ministering to their needs.

   c. At the height of His atoning work while dying on the cross, Jesus did not neglect the needs of His own family. While He was suffering, He instructed the apostle John to care for His mother (Jn. 19:26-27).

   d. Finally, Jesus did not fall prey to thinking only in terms of short-range goals. He carefully followed the program set forth by the Father. He strategically planned three years of ministry to be followed by each generation winning others and teaching them all that He had taught the original disciples.

Complete Day One, question 4 and Day Two, question 1 in the Home Study Guide.

III. THE GIFT OF TEACHING

The Analytical Person

A. Definition

1. The one with the motivational gift of teaching has the ability to search out and clarify truth.

2. He is given to much detailed study and research.

B. The Greek Term

1. In the Greek New Testament the word for this gift is based upon the verb *didasko*. In Classical Greek this word spoke of the action of a teacher whose concern was to develop the abilities of his pupils and to impart to them his knowledge and skill.

2. In the Christian concept, however, this word takes on a different meaning. Rather than emphasizing the communication of knowledge and skills, it looks instead toward instructing people in how to live.

3. The objective of the teacher is always to point out the will of God according to the Scriptures. The goal is not so much the development of the student's abilities, but the promotion of obedience to God's will.

C. Characteristics

1. Strengths

   a. The teacher has a strong desire for in-depth knowledge of the truths of Scripture and other related subjects.

   b. The teacher has the ability to clarify and explain biblical truth to others.

   c. The teacher presents truth in an organized, systematic way and is concerned to integrate all new truth into an established system.

   d. The teacher enjoys the world of books and ideas more than that of people. He may, therefore, appear to be a loner.

   e. The teacher places great emphasis on factual accuracy. He emphasizes the careful and accurate use of words in particular. This extends beyond biblical and theological terms to the use of language in general.

f. The teacher has a great concern for the careful use of Scripture with proper regard for its context. In this regard, the teacher is a guardian of right doctrine and is greatly disturbed when he sees others misuse Scripture by taking it out of context.

g. The teacher believes his gift is foundational to all the other gifts.

h. The teacher insists on validating any new truth from Scripture. He prefers biblical illustrations to those drawn from other spheres of life.

i. The teacher insists on knowing the source of authority for a new concept. He will personally research it before accepting its validity. As a result, the teacher usually documents extensively when he speaks. Another result is that the teacher is able to suspend judgment on a question almost indefinitely until he can research it and form his own conclusions from Scripture.

2. Weaknesses

a. Sometimes the teacher is more interested in factual details than the practical application of truth. The exhortation gift which has the opposite emphasis serves to provide a balance in this regard.

b. The teacher may end up living in an ivory tower because he loves research more than the actual presentation of the truth.

c. Pride of knowledge is a contant pitfall for those with a teaching gift.

d. The teacher's concern for detail may appear unnecessary to his hearers leading to boredom or even frustration and confusion.

e. The teacher faces the danger of depending upon learning and scholarship alone for his understanding of Scripture. He may at times find himself guilty of not relying upon the teaching and illuminating ministry of the Holy Spirit.

f. The teacher's desire to validate authority for a new concept can seem like intellectual snobbery. At times he can appear to be insubordinate because of wanting to check things out before he moves ahead on a project.

g. The teacher's ability to suspend judgment on unresearched issues can be seen as indecisiveness or excessive dependence upon the intellect.

h. The teacher may discount the practical lessons learned by others through the experiences of life. As a result, he can close himself to the insights of people with little formal education.

i. The teacher's insistence on strict factual accuracy may cause him to "throw out the baby with the bath water," i.e., a small factual error can cause a teacher to reject an otherwise excellent teaching from someone else.

D. Areas for Growth

The following scriptures provide insights that can balance the weaknesses of the teaching gift.

1. Following the passage where he lists the motivational gifts, Paul tells us, "Never to be lacking in zeal, but keep your spiritual fervor, serving the Lord" (Ro. 12:11). This verse is very relevant to the teacher. He must constantly remember that understanding truth is not the goal of the Christian life. Knowledge is simply the means to attain the goal of developing our relationship with Jesus Christ.

2. In Proverbs 3:5 we read, "Trust in the Lord with all your heart and lean not on your own understanding." The teacher must always ensure that his efforts

III. TEACHING

1 Corinthians 8:1
Now about food sacrificed to idols: We know that we all possess knowledge. Knowledge puffs up, but love builds up.

Matthew 28:19-20
Therefore go and make disciples of all nations, baptizing them in the name of the Father and of the Son and of the Holy Spirit. ²⁰ and teaching them to obey everything I have commanded you. And surely I will be with you always, to the very end of the age.

are directed toward trusting God. He must avoid the pitfall of living only in accordance with his intellectual understanding of life.

3. The teacher must constantly strive to grow in the love of Christ so that he may edify others. He must be aware of the fact that growth in knowledge alone only leads to pride (1 Cor. 8:1).

E.   Biblical Example

Matthew (the author of the Gospel of Matthew)

1. The teacher's love of a systematic approach to truth can be seen in the arrangement of Matthew's gospel. It is the most systematic book in the New Testament.

2. Matthew, the teacher, in his desire to keep things in context, groups the teaching of Jesus according to topic. For example, in chapter 13, he gathers together several parables of Christ about the Kingdom of heaven. In Matthew chapters 5-7, he gathers together Christ's ethical teachings in what we call the Sermon on the Mount.

3. The teacher's belief that his gift is foundational can be seen in Matthew's decision to record Christ's use of the word "teach" in the Great Commission (Mt. 28:19-20).

4. The teacher's desire to integrate all truth with a previously established system and to provide documentation can be seen in the fact that Matthew quotes more Old Testament scripture than any other gospel writer. He constantly shows how the gospel completes the message of the Old Testament.

5. The teacher's love of research can be seen in the care Matthew took to research the genealogy of Christ (Mt. 1:1-17).

III. TEACHING

John 1:37-38
When the two disciples heard him say this, they followed Jesus. ³⁸ Turning around, Jesus saw them following and asked, "What do you want?"
They said, "Rabbi" (which means Teacher), "where are you staying?"

John 3:2
He came to Jesus at night and said, "Rabbi, we know you are a teacher who has come from God. For no one could perform the miraculous signs you are doing if God were not with him."

Matthew 5:1-2
Now when he saw the crowds, he went up on a mountainside and sat down. His disciples came to him, ²and he began to teach them.

Mark 1:21
They went to Capernaum, and when the Sabbath came, Jesus went into the synagogue and began to teach.

Luke 4:15
He taught in their synagogues, and everyone praised him.

Luke 2:46-47
After three days they found him in the temple courts, sitting among the teachers, listening to them and asking them questions. ⁴⁷Everyone who heard him was amazed at his understanding and his answers.

Mark 12:26-27
Now about the dead rising—have you not read in the book of Moses, in the account of the bush, how God said to him, 'I am the God of Abraham, the God of Isaac, and the God of Jacob'? ²⁷He is not the God of the dead, but of the living. You are badly mistaken!"

John 7:16
Jesus answered, "My teaching is not my own. It comes from him who sent me."

F. Christ's Example

1. The following instances indicate that Jesus possessed the motivatonal gift of teaching:

   a. Christ was called a teacher by His disciples and also by the religious leader, Nicodemus (Jn. 1:37-38, 3:2).

   b. Christ spent a good deal of time teaching people (Mt. 5:1-2; Mk. 1:21; Lk. 4:15).

   c. Like a teacher, Jesus possessed the ability to clarify truth. Even at a very early age, the theological experts of His day were astounded at His understanding of truth (Lk. 2:46-47).

   d. Jesus was concerned for the accurate use of words. In one instance, in order to prove the doctrine of the resurrection, He rested His entire argument upon the use of the present tense when God said, "I *am* the God of Abraham." Based on this fact, He pointed out that God is not the God of the dead, but of the living because of the use of the present tense in this quotation from Exodus 3:6 (Mk. 12:26-27).

   e. In John 7:16, Christ manifested the teacher's desire to make clear the source of His authority when He said, "My teaching is not my own. It comes from Him who sent me."

2. The example of Christ helps the teacher balance the weaknesses of his gift:

   a. Although Christ presented truth with clarity of detail, He never ignored the importance of applying it to practical Christian living.

   b. Christ never became proud of His knowledge. He constantly pointed to God the Father as His source of authority.

   c. He never isolated Himself from others. He constantly developed new relationships with those to whom He ministered.

IV. EXHORTATION

Complete Day Two, question 2 and Day Three questions 1 and 2 in the Home Study Guide.

IV. THE GIFT OF EXHORTATION

The Encouraging Person

A. Definition

1. The one who possesses the motivational gift of exhortation has the ability to encourage others to grow spiritually.

2. The exhorter can be distinguished from the teacher in that he validates truth by studying the practical experience of others.

B. The Greek Term

In the Greek New Testament, exhortation, *paraklesis* (from the verb, *parakaleō*) has a rich variety of meaning:

1. It can involve not only encouraging someone, but also pleading with them to follow God's will and obey His word.

2. It can mean giving comfort to those in distress and admonition or warning to those in danger of abandoning the Christian way.

3. The one who exhorts others often acts as a Christian counselor.

4. The exhorter is also one who stands beside to plead another's case, hence, this word includes the concept of intercessory prayer. Exhorters are to pray for those they encourage.

5. The one with the gift of *paraklēsis* gives others strength to serve God and thus this word comes from the same root that is translated, "comforter" or "counselor" with reference to the ministry of the Holy Spirit (Jn. 14:15-17, 26).

John 14:15-17
"If you love me, you will obey what I command. ¹⁶ And I will ask the Father, and he will give you another Counselor to be with you forever—¹⁷ the Spirit of truth. The world cannot accept him, because it neither sees him nor knows him. But you know him, for he lives with you and will be in you.

John 14:26 (KJV)
But the Comforter, which is the Holy Ghost, whom the Father will send in my name, he shall teach you all things, and bring all things to your remembrance, whatsoever I have said unto you.

IV. EXHORTATION

C. Characteristics

1. Strengths

   a. The exhorter is one who listens, encourages, admonishes, gives advice, and acts as an ally. His gift is that of the Christian counselor.

   b. The exhorter stirs up others to action. His message is directed therefore toward the goal of spiritual growth. He is God's cheerleader.

   c. The exhorter loves to teach the practical application of Scripture rather than just the factual understanding of truth like the teacher.

   d. The exhorter has a very positive attitude and outlook on life and is usually greatly appreciated. He places a strong emphasis on God's grace and believes that we can do all things through Christ.

   e. The exhorter sees all suffering and hardship as an opportunity for Christian growth.

   f. For the exhorter, truth is truth regardless of its source, whether it be the Scriptures or practical experience.

   g. The exhorter loves to give specific and practical prescriptions to overcome problems. His constant refrain is, "Here is God's answer. . . ."

   h. The exhorter is person-centered and loves to counsel individuals on a one-to-one basis. Unlike the prophet, who is virtually unaware of his listeners, the exhorter is very aware of his listeners and needs to know that they are giving him their full attention.

2. Weaknesses

   a. Because of his insistence that suffering provides an opportunity for growth, the exhorter may appear hard and callous toward the feelings of others.

IV. EXHORTATION

b. The exhorter may oversimplify complex issues, set unrealistic goals, and give premature advice because of his desire to provide practical steps for Christian growth.

c. The exhorter will sometimes take Scripture out of context to support a valid point he wishes to emphasize. He is directly opposite to the teacher in this regard.

d. The exhorter feeds on success and, therefore, often becomes impatient in helping people who do not show quick improvement.

e. Because of his constant desire to help others grow spiritually and the time required for counseling individuals, the exhorter's family may suffer neglect.

D. Areas for Growth

The following scriptures provide insights that the exhorter should heed in order to balance the weaknesses of his gift:

1. The words of Romans 12:12: "Be joyful in hope, patient in affliction, faithful in prayer" apply to the exhorter who can become impatient with those who fail to show rapid progress.

2. Because of his tendency to take Scripture out of context, the exhorter needs to hear Paul's words in 2 Timothy 2:15: "Do your best to present yourself to God as one approved, a workman who does not need to be ashamed and *who correctly handles the word of truth*" (emphasis added).

3. Because of the tendency to ignore the needs of his own family, exhorters should pay attention to Paul's words in 1 Timothy 5:8: "If anyone does not provide for his relatives, and especially for his immediate family, he has denied the faith and is worse than an unbeliever."

IV. EXHORTATION

Acts 14:21-22
They preached the good news in that city and won a large number of disciples. Then they returned to Lystra, Iconium and Antioch, [22] strengthening the disciples and encouraging them to remain true to the faith. "We must go through many hardships to enter the kingdom of God," they said.

Acts 20:1-2
When the uproar had ended, Paul sent for the disciples and, after encouraging them, said good-by and set out for Macedonia. [2] He traveled through that area, speaking many words of encouragement to the people, and finally arrived in Greece.

Ephesians 4:1
As a prisoner for the Lord, then, I urge you to live a life worthy of the calling you have received.

1 Thessalonians 5:14
And we urge you, brothers, warn those who are idle, encourage the timid, help the weak, be patient with everyone.

Colossians 1:28-29
We proclaim him, admonishing and teaching everyone with all wisdom, so that we may present everyone perfect in Christ. [29] To this end I labor, struggling with all his energy, which so powerfully works in me.

Acts 11:23
When he arrived and saw the evidence of the grace of God, he was glad and encouraged them all to remain true to the Lord with all their hearts.

Matthew 11:28-30
"Come to me, all you who are weary and burdened, and I will give you rest. [29] Take my yoke upon you and learn from me, for I am gentle and humble in heart, and you will find rest for your souls. [30] For my yoke is easy and my burden is light."

E. Biblical Examples

1. The apostle Paul is a prime example of one who exhibited the motivational gift of exhortation.

   a. The Greek term for this gift of exhortation is applied to Paul's ministry several times in the Book of Acts (14:21-22, 16:40, 20:1-2).

   b. Throughout his epistles, Paul often uses a related term when he calls upon believers to follow the Lord. For example, in Romans 12:1 he says, "Therefore, I urge you, brothers, . . ." the word *urge* in this verse is the same word Paul uses with reference to the motivational gift of exhortation. We find a similar pattern in many other passages where Paul exhorts his readers to follow the Lord more faithfully (Eph. 4:1; Phil. 4:2; 1 Thes. 5:14; 1 Tim. 2:1).

   c. In Colossians 1:28-29, Paul sets forth the goal of every exhorter with regard to his ministry: "That we may present everyone perfect in Christ."

2. The Book of Acts makes it evident that Barnabas also possessed this gift.

   a. In Acts 4:36 we are told that the meaning of the name, Barnabas is "Son of encouragement" using the Greek word for exhortation.

   b. Acts 11:23 speaks of Barnabas doing a work of exhortation. Acts 14:22 speaks of both Paul and Barnabas exhorting others.

F. Christ's Example

1. Jesus Christ perfectly exemplifies the qualities of one with the gift of exhortation:

   a. He calls upon all believers to come to Him to receive rest and encouragement (Mt. 11:28-30).

   b. In 1 John 2:1, Christ is called our *paraklēton* or advocate using a word from the same root as that which describes the gift of exhortation.

IV. EXHORTATION

Mark 7:21-22
For from within, out of men's hearts, come evil thoughts, sexual immorality, theft, murder, adultery, ²²greed, malice, deceit, lewdness, envy, slander, arrogance and folly.

Mark 6:1-2
Jesus left there and went to his home town, accompanied by his disciples. ²When the Sabbath came, he began to teach in the synagogue, and many who heard him were amazed. "Where did this man get these things?" they asked. "What's this wisdom that has been given him, that he even does miracles!"

Hebrews 2:17-18
For this reason he had to be made like his brothers in every way, in order that he might become a merciful and faithful high priest in service to God, and that he might make atonement for the sins of the people. ¹⁸Because he himself suffered when he was tempted, he is able to help those who are being tempted.

c. In John chapter 14, Jesus promised He would send another comforter or *paraklētos* in the person of the Holy Spirit. It is obvious from the context that the first *parakletos* was the Lord Himself, the great Encourager.

d. In 2 Thessalonians 2:16, we read that through the Father and the Lord Jesus Christ, we have received "eternal encouragement (*paraklēsin*) and good hope."

2. As in all things, Jesus Christ is our example of how to exercise the gift of exhortation without its accompanying weaknesses:

a. Although Christ encouraged people to spiritual growth, He did not oversimplify complex issues or establish unrealistic goals. He understood the depth of human depravity (Mk. 7:21-22).

b. Christ never used Scripture out of context. Rather, He was a master of correct interpretation. His ability to illuminate the full meaning of the biblical text often astonished His hearers (Mt. 22:41-46; Mk. 6:1-2).

c. Although Christ realized the importance of suffering as an opportunity for spiritual growth, He was able to minister with great empathy, gentleness, and understanding. He is our great high priest, the one who is touched with the feelings of our infirmities (Heb. 2:17-18, 5:2).

d. Christ showed great persistence in working closely with individuals who did not respond readily or quickly to His teaching. We think particularly of the Twelve and how they failed so often to understand what Jesus was trying to teach them (Mk. 8:17-21).

Complete Day Three, questions 3-5 in the Home Study Guide.

V. THE GIFT OF GIVING

The Generous Person

A. Definition

1. The one with the motivational gift of giving has the constant desire and most often the ability to give generously. This person approaches all of life in terms of giving.

2. God often blesses this individual with abundant financial and material resources enabling him to contribute generously to the Lord's work.

B. The Greek Term

1. The Greek word for this gift, *metadidomi* means to share what you have with someone else.

2. In Romans 12:8, those with the gift of giving are told to give with *haplotēs* or simplicity, sincerity, uprightness, and frankness. This means that they are to give with singleness of heart, having no mixed motives and no regrets. Those who give like this do so for the joy of giving for its own sake.

C. Characteristics

1. Strengths

   a. The giver is a thrifty person and a good manager of money. As a result, he usually has more resources available for the Lord's work.

   b. The giver has insight into when and to whom he should give. He is able to discern which opportunities provide good investments for the work of the kingdom. He is often able to discover needs that others may overlook.

   c. The giver is willing to sacrifice personally in order to give more.

   d. The giver wants all of the credit for his gift to go to God.

e. The giver supports the ministry of others and yet wants to participate in that ministry significantly and to feel a vital part of it.

f. The giver likes to give in a way that will encourage others to give as well.

g. The giver desires to give anonymously in obedience to the Lord's prompting. His greatest joy comes in discovering that his gift provided an answer to someone's prayers. Because of his desire to depend upon the Lord's guidance, the giver refuses to be pressured into giving.

h. Because all of God's work requires financial and material resources, the gift of giving is essential to the work of the kingdom.

2. Weaknesses

a. The giver tends to be cause-oriented rather than people-oriented. For this reason, he tends to be attracted to tangible projects like building programs rather than ministering to the needs of people.

b. The giver can be judgmental in his attitude toward others who are poor financial managers. As a result, he may not make a good financial counselor.

c. Givers face the danger of shortchanging the needs of their own family by acting independently of their spouses. They often assume that their family has the same sacrificial spirit that they do.

d. Givers always face the danger of giving for wrong motives. They need to be careful of self-aggrandizement or the manipulation of the organizations to which they give. It is for the reason that Paul exhorts them to give with simplicity i.e., unmixed motives.

e. The giver desires to see his investment for the kingdom managed properly. For this reason he is often viewed as desiring to manipulate the ministry or ministries he supports.

f. The giver's discernment regarding investments that would be most beneficial for the kingdom and his refusal to respond to pressure may cause him to seem selfish and ungenerous to those who do not know him well.

D. Areas for Growth

The following are some scriptural exhortations that all givers should heed in order to balance the weaknesses of their gift.

1. Givers should heed the words of Romans 12:13, "Share with God's people who are in need. Practice hospitality." These words emphasize to the giver the need to be people-oriented rather than simply project-oriented.

2. Paul's exhortation in 1 Timothy 5:8 concerning caring for those in one's own family is particularly applicable to the person with the gift of giving.

3. In Matthew 6:2-4, Jesus taught us to give secretly in order to avoid the sin of pride. This exhortation is particularly applicable to those with the gift of giving.

E. Biblical Examples

1. Abraham manifested some of the characteristics of one with the motivational gift of giving:

a. He was a good financial manager and as a result, accumulated large resources because of God's blessing (Gen. 24:1, 34-35).

b. That he was willing to sacrifice everything to God is shown by his willingness to sacrifice his only son, Isaac (Gen. 22:1-3).

---

1 Timothy 5:8
If anyone does not provide for his relatives, and especially for his immediate family, he has denied the faith and is worse than an unbeliever.

Matthew 6:2-4
"So when you give to the needy, do not announce it with trumpets, as the hypocrites do in the synagogues and on the streets, to be honored by men. I tell you the truth, they have received their reward in full. ³But when you give to the needy, do not let your left hand know what your right hand is doing, ⁴so that your giving may be in secret. Then your Father, who sees what is done in secret, will reward you."

Genesis 24:1
Abraham was now old and well advanced in years, and the LORD had blessed him in every way.

Genesis 24:34-35
So he said, "I am Abraham's servant. ³⁵The LORD has blessed my master abundantly, and he has become wealthy. He has given him sheep and cattle, silver and gold, menservants and maidservants, and camels and donkeys."

Genesis 22:1-3
Some time later God tested Abraham. He said to him, "Abraham!"

"Here I am," he replied.

²Then God said, "Take your son, your only son Isaac, whom you love, and go to the region of Moriah. Sacrifice him there as a burnt offering on one of the mountains I will tell you about."

³Early the next morning Abraham got up and saddled his donkey. He took with him two of his servants and his son Isaac. When he had cut enough wood for the burnt offering, he set out for the place God had told him about.

c. Abraham manifested a spirit of great generosity in his dealings with his nephew, Lot (Gen. 13:1-11).

2. Jospeh of Arimathea manifested this gift in giving his own new tomb for the burial of Jesus Christ (Mt. 27:57-60).

F. Christ's Example

1. The Lord Jesus often manifested the gift of giving especially through the things He taught:

a. We know that Christ was very concerned with good financial stewardship as indicated by the Parable of the Talents and the Parable of the Pounds (Mt. 25:14-30; Lk. 19:11-27).

b. Christ believed in giving in secret so as to avoid the danger of pride as He taught in Matthew 6:2-4.

c. Christ's sacrifice on Calvary serves as a tremendous example of sacrificial giving. He gave up the glories of heaven and became poor for our sake that we might enjoy eternal life (2 Cor. 8:9).

2. In the following ways, Christ can serve as an example to assist givers in overcoming the weaknesses associated with their gift:

a. Throughout His ministry, Christ was people-oriented, taking time for the needs of individuals. His days were filled with ministering to children, individuals, and crowds.

b. Christ constantly sought to promote the glory of His Father rather than to exalt Himself (Jn. 17:4). By following His example, the giver can be protected from the danger of placing himself in a superior position.

Complete Day Four, questions 1-4 in the Home Study Guide.

Matthew 6:2-4
"So when you give to the needy, do not announce it with trumpets, as the hypocrites do in the synagogues and on the streets, to be honored by men. I tell you the truth, they have received their reward in full. ³But when you give to the needy, do not let your left hand know what your right hand is doing, ⁴so that your giving may be in secret. Then your Father, who sees what is done in secret, will reward you.

2 Corinthians 8:9
For you know the grace of our Lord Jesus Christ, that though he was rich, yet for your sakes he became poor, so that you through his poverty might become rich.

John 17:4
I have brought you glory on earth by completing the work you gave me to do.

VI. ADMINISTRATION

VI. THE GIFT OF ADMINISTRATION

The Organizing Person

A. Definition

Those who possess the motivational gift of administration have the ability to coordinate people, resources, and schedules to achieve goals.

B. The Greek Term

1. In the Greek New Testament, the word used in Romans 12:8 for leadership or administration is *proistēmi* which means literally the one who stands before others.

2. This word applies to a large variety of leadership roles such as being the head of a village, the guardian of a child, the superintendent of a trade guild, or the chief of a company of musicians. It is used in reference to elders who "rule" the church in Paul's first letter to Timothy (5:17). It also carries the concept of supporting or caring for people such as a father does for the members of his family (1 Tim. 3:4-5, 12).

C. Characteristics

1. Strengths

   a. The administrator sees overall goals and objectives and the steps needed to reach them. Unlike servers, he likes long-range plans.

   b. The administrator likes to see all of the parts of a project come together.

   c. Administrators will take up leadership where none previously existed i.e., they have initiative.

   d. The administrator likes to delegate responsibility and knows what to delegate and what not to

1 Timothy 5:17
The elders who direct the affairs of the church well are worthy of double honor, especially those whose work is preaching and teaching.

1 Timothy 3:4-5
He must manage his own family well and see that his children obey him with proper respect. 5(If anyone does not know how to manage his own family, how can he take care of God's church?)

1 Timothy 3:12
A deacon must be the husband of but one wife and must manage his children and his household well.

VI. ADMINISTRATION

delegate. Administrators also keep careful track of what's going on even though others may be doing the work for them.

e. Administrators have an unusual ability to withstand criticism and opposition.

f. Administrators are people of action who like to keep the ball rolling. They are not easily sidetracked from getting the job accomplished.

g. The administrator has the ability to discern the gifts of people and to put them to effective use.

h. Administrators have the ability to inspire and challenge those under them to complete the task at hand with the appropriate use of praise and approval.

i. Administrators are willing to sacrifice personally to whatever degree is necessary to accomplish the goal. They inspire others because of their willingness to sacrifice to accomplish the goal.

2. Weaknesses

a. Administrators are task-oriented rather than people-oriented and often appear to use people to accomplish selfish ambitions. They are also prone to overloading people because they keep their eyes on the task and not on the personal needs of their workers.

b. The administrator's ability to endure reaction may cause him to appear insensitive to the needs of people.

c. Administrators face the temptation to respond in kind to the harsh criticism and opposition they may face.

d. The administrator must always take care not to trust exclusively in his ability to plan. He must learn to depend upon God for direction.

VI. ADMINISTRATION

e. Administrators tend to be weak in listening skills and can, therefore, ignore the good ideas of others.

f. Administrators often fail to explain to the individual worker how his contribution fits in with the whole. As a result, workers may feel little or no ownership in the project.

D. Areas for Growth

The following are scriptural admonitions that particularly apply to the weaknesses of administrators:

1. Paul's words in Romans 12:14, "Bless those who persecute you; bless and do not curse" appear to be directed particularly toward administrators. In their ability to withstand criticism they face the temptation of retaliation.

2. The emphasis on love clearly set forth in First Corinthians chapter 13 must constantly be borne in mind by the administrator. He is often so wrapped up in accomplishing the project, that he forgets the needs of the people involved.

3. The administrator needs to keep in mind the teaching of Philippians 2:3-4, "Do nothing out of selfish ambition or vain conceit, but in humility consider others better than yourselves. Each of you should look not only to your own interests, but also to the interests of others." The administrator needs to be open to the ideas of others, recognizing the value of their gifts.

E. Biblical Examples

1. Moses seems to have possessed the gift of administration. Witness his obvious ability to organize a whole nation and lead them through forty years of nomadic adventures. Note as well his meek reaction to the continual opposition he faced (Nu. 12:3, 14:1-5).

2. Nehemiah is perhaps the outstanding administrator in Scripture for some of the following reasons:

Numbers 12:3
Now Moses was a very humble man, more humble than anyone else on the face of the earth.

Numbers 14:1-5
That night all the people of the community raised their voices and wept aloud. ²All the Israelites grumbled against Moses and Aaron, and the whole assembly said to them, "If only we had died in Egypt! Or in this desert! ³Why is the LORD bringing us to this land only to let us fall by the sword? Our wives and children will be taken as plunder. Wouldn't it be better for us to go back to Egypt?" ⁴And they said to each other, "We should choose a leader and go back to Egypt."
⁵Then Moses and Aaron fell facedown in front of the whole Israelite assembly gathered there.

VI. ADMINISTRATION

Nehemiah 2:6-8
Then the king, with the queen sitting beside him, asked me, "How long will your journey take, and when will you get back?" It pleased the king to send me; so I set a time.

⁷ I also said to him, "If it pleases the king, may I have letters to the governors of Trans-Euphrates, so that they will provide me safe-conduct until I arrive in Judah? ⁸ And may I have a letter to Asaph, keeper of the king's forest, so he will give me timber to make beams for the gates of the citadel by the temple and for the city wall and for the residence I will occupy?" And because the gracious hand of my God was upon me, the king granted my requests.

Nehemiah 4:12-13
Then the Jews who lived near them came and told us ten times over, "Wherever you turn, they will attack us." ¹³ Therefore I stationed some of the people behind the lowest points of the wall at the exposed places, posting them by families, with their swords, spears and bows.

Nehemiah 2:17-18
Then I said to them, "You see the trouble we are in: Jerusalem lies in ruins, and its gates have been burned with fire. Come, let us rebuild the wall of Jerusalem, and we will no longer be in disgrace." ¹⁸ I also told them about the gracious hand of my God upon me and what the king had said to me.

They replied, "Let us start rebuilding." So they began this good work.

a. He had the ability to set objectives and determine goals. This is illustrated by his plan which he presented to the king for rebuilding Jerusalem (Neh. 2:6-8).

b. He had the initiative to take up leadership where none existed to accomplish a task that needed to be done (Neh. 1).

c. Nehemiah had the ability to delegate responsibility and to keep track of the overall project. This is evident from the way he organized the people to work on the wall (Neh. ch. 3; 4:12-13).

d. Nehemiah had an unusual ability to withstand criticism and opposition (Neh. 6:1-13).

e. Nehemiah was a man of action who kept the ball rolling and was not easily sidetracked (Neh. 6:1-8).

f. Nehemiah had the ability to challenge and inspire those under him (Neh. 2:17-18; 4:14).

g. Nehemiah set an example of self-sacrifice in order to accomplish the goal (Neh. 5:14-18).

F. Christ's Example

1. Our Lord Jesus Christ gave evidence of possessing the characteristics of an administrator:

a. He carefully planned a strategy that involved twelve people who in turn would train many others to literally carry His message around the world throughout all generations.

b. In Mark 6:39-40, we see Jesus organizing the five thousand so that they could be fed with a minimum of confusion.

c. Christ's constant battles with the Pharisees indicate that He had the ability to withstand opposition and criticism.

Mark 6:6-13

Then Jesus went around teaching from village to village. 7 Calling the Twelve to him, he sent them out two by two and gave them authority over evil spirits.

8 These were his instructions: "Take nothing for the journey except a staff—no bread, no bag, no money in your belts. 9 Wear sandals but not an extra tunic. 10 Whenever you enter a house, stay there until you leave that town. 11 And if any place will not welcome you or listen to you, shake the dust off your feet when you leave, as a testimony against them."

12 They went out and preached that people should repent. 13 They drove out many demons and anointed many sick people with oil and healed them.

John 4:34

"My food," said Jesus, "is to do the will of him who sent me and to finish his work."

d. Christ's organization of His disciples, sending them out two-by-two on preaching and healing missions gives evidence of His abilities as an administrator (Mk. 6:6-13; Lk. 10:1-16).

2. The following are some ways in which administrators can overcome their weaknesses by following the example of Christ:

a. Throughout His ministry, Christ was people-centered. He spent time ministering to individuals as well as to the crowds.

b. Christ set an example for us in responding to criticism. At His trial, He did not open His mouth to defend Himself despite the fact that the charges against Him were totally false (Mk. 15:1-5).

c. The prayer life of Christ serves as a constant reminder that He sought the Father's will. This sets an example for the administrator showing him that he should not get too wrapped up in his own plans and schedules without consulting the Lord's direction (Jn. 4:34).

Complete Day Four, questions 5-6 in the Home Study Guide.

VII. THE GIFT OF MERCY

The Compassionate Person

A. Definition:

Those who possess the motivational gift of mercy have the ability to identify with and comfort those in distress. They feel deeply the hurts of other people.

B. The Greek Term

1. To have mercy (Greek, *eleeō*) means to identify with the misery of another enough so as to take concrete action to alleviate their sufferings.

VII. MERCY

Titus 3:5
He saved us, not because of righteous things we had done, but because of his mercy. He saved us through the washing of rebirth and renewal by the Holy Spirit.

Jude 22
Be merciful to those who doubt.

2. This term is also used to speak of God's forgiveness and clemency with reference to His gracious offer of salvation through Christ (Tit. 3:5).

3. This latter fact suggests that the one with the gift of mercy is able to minister to others the gracious assurance of God's forgiveness through Christ (Jude 22).

4. Paul says in Romans 12:8 that this gift should be exercised with cheerfulness or *hilarotēs* so that the merciful one will not be overwhelmed with grief in his identification with the hurts of others.

C. Characteristics

1. Strengths

   a. The merciful person is deeply concerned about people on a one-to-one basis. He finds himself constantly attracted to those who are in distress. There is an intuitive ability to detect hurt feelings in others. Merciful people are feelers.

   b. The merciful person has a special sensitivity to emotional needs and is able to respond to others with tenderness, kindness, and compassion. These people often communicate through touching as well as kind words.

   c. The merciful person avoids actions and words that will hurt the feelings of others including disciplinary and administrative decisions. In this regard, he is the opposite of the administrator.

   d. Merciful people place a strong emphasis on prayer and the ministry of healing in the body of Christ.

   e. Merciful people are the most tolerant of all Christians with references to differences in people's race, color, and religion. They are able to communicate unconditional love better than any other person.

f. Merciful people reach out sacrificially to meet the needs of others. Servers are also sacrificial in nature, but their sacrifice is directed toward getting the task accomplished rather than ministering to the emotional needs of people.

2. Weaknesses

   a. Merciful people can sometimes become too emotionally involved with others and thus lose their sense of objectivity.

   b. The merciful person can often become closed in spirit toward others who are insensitive or insincere.

   c. Merciful people avoid situations involving stress, conflict, and firmness. This can make them appear indecisive. Their unwillingness to speak the *truth* in love can cause problems at times when a loving rebuke is necessary.

   d. Because of their strong emotional involvement with the one who is hurting, there is the danger of improper involvement with the opposite sex.

   e. Because merciful people identify so completely with the sufferings of others, they are subject to depression.

   f. Because they are so afraid of hurting others, merciful people can sometimes repress healthy, negative feelings. This can cause them to lash out when they cannot hold their feelings in any longer.

   g. Because they are so sensitive, merciful people tend to be wounded easily by others.

   h. Merciful people sometimes ignore the needs of their own family because of their deep concern for others.

   i. Their eagerness to help can sometimes be misinterpreted by others as a desire to stick their noses into other people's business.

VII. MERCY

j. Their eagerness to help can also cause merciful people to short-circuit God's process of discipline. Struggle is painful but sometimes, it is necessary.

k. Because they feel intensely, the merciful can fall into the trap of living by their feelings instead of by the truth.

D. Areas for Growth

The following are some insights from Scripture that will assist merciful people in overcoming the weaknesses associated with their gift:

1. In Romans 12:15, Paul says, "Rejoice with those who rejoice; mourn with those who mourn". It would seem these words are particularly applicable to the merciful. They tend to remain on the mourning side of things. They need also to rejoice with others.

Luke 17:3
If your brother sins, rebuke him, and if he repents, forgive him.

2. The merciful need to hear Paul's words in Ephesians 4:15 by learning how to speak the *truth* in love. There are times when rebuke is necessary as, for example, when your brother sins against you (Lk. 17:3).

3. Merciful people must realize that, at times, God allows suffering and struggle in order to discipline His children and mold them into the image of Christ (Heb. 12:4-13). They must learn not to be "rescuers" in certain situations.

Matthew 4:4
Jesus answered, "It is written: 'Man does not live on bread alone, but on every word that comes from the mouth of God.'"

4. Merciful people need to learn not to live by their feelings alone, but to depend upon the Word of God (Mt. 4:4).

E. Biblical Examples

1. Luke, the writer of the third Gospel, seems to have been a person with the motivational gift of mercy:

a. His gospel shows an unusual interest in people. One scholar has calculated that Luke names 110 different people in the Book of Acts alone.

b. We see from his gospel that Luke is attracted to people in distress. His book contains parables about the rich man and Lazarus, the prodigal son, and the Good Samaritan.

c. Luke's interest in the ministry of healing is evident. He uses frequent examples of this ministry at work in both the Gospel of Luke and the Book of Acts.

2. With the exception of Jesus Christ, the Good Samaritan is perhaps the most outstanding example of a merciful person in Scripture (Lk. 10:25-37).

a. The merciful person's empathy for the needs of others is emphasized in this story. The Scripture says the Good Samaritan took *pity* on the man by the roadside. Jesus is the principal person in Scripture to whom this same type of pity is attributed.

b. The Good Samaritan's interest in the ministry of healing is evidenced by the comprehensive steps he took to bring about the complete healing of the injured man.

c. The Good Samaritan manifested unconditional love toward a stranger. History reveals that there was great hatred between the Samaritans and the Jews. But this man overcame whatever feelings he might have had to help someone in distress

d. We see in the Good Samaritan the sacrificial nature of the merciful person. He was willing to provide financially for the individual until he was well.

F. Christ's Example

1. There can be little doubt that Jesus Christ is the most merciful person portrayed in the Scriptures:

a. Hebrews 2:17 calls Jesus Christ our *merciful* high priest.

Luke 10:25-37

On one occasion an expert in the law stood up to test Jesus, "Teacher," he asked, "what must I do to inherit eternal life?"

²⁶"What is written in the Law?" he replied, "How do you read it?"

²⁷He answered: "'Love the Lord your God with all your heart and with all your soul and with all your strength and with all your mind'; and, 'Love your neighbor as yourself.'"

²⁸"You have answered correctly," Jesus replied. "Do this and you will live."

²⁹But he wanted to justify himself, so he asked Jesus, "And who is my neighbor?"

³⁰In reply Jesus said: "A man was going down from Jerusalem to Jericho, when he fell into the hands of robbers. They stripped him of his clothes, beat him and went away, leaving him half dead. ³¹A priest happened to be going down the same road, and when he saw the man, he passed by on the other side. ³²So too, a Levite, when he came to the place and saw him, passed by on the other side. ³³But a Samaritan, as he traveled, came where the man was; and when he saw him, he took pity on him. ³⁴He went to him and bandaged his wounds, pouring on oil and wine. Then he put the man on his own donkey, took him to an inn and took care of him. ³⁵The next day he took out two silver coins and gave them to the innkeeper. 'Look after him,' he said, 'and when I return, I will reimburse you for any extra expense you may have.'

³⁶"Which of these three do you think was a neighbor to the main who fell into the hands of robbers?"

³⁷The expert in the law replied, "The one who had mercy on him."

Jesus told him, "Go and do likewise."

Matthew 9:36
When he saw the crowds, he had compassion on them, because they were harassed and helpless, like sheep without a shepherd.

Matthew 14:14
When Jesus landed and saw a large crowd, he had compassion on them and healed their sick.

Mark 1:41
Filled with compassion, Jesus reached out his hand and touched the man. "I am willing," he said "Be clean!"

Matthew 16:23
Jesus turned and said to Peter, "Out of my sight, Satan! You are a stumbling block to me; you do not have in mind the things of God, but the things of men."

b. In Philippians chapter 2, we read of Christ's total identification with the pain and suffering of man's fallen condition (Phil. 2:5-8).

c. The Scriptures constantly speak of Jesus being full of compassion. The type of compassion spoken of involves deep identification with those who are suffering (Mt. 9:36, 14:14; Mk. 1:41).

2. Christ serves as an example to the merciful person in overcoming the weaknesses associated with their gift:

a. Jesus rebuked Peter and the other disciples when it was necessary. He could be firm if the situation required it (Mt. 16:23).

b. Although Christ felt deeply for the needs of others, He never came to the place where He began to live by His feelings. In fact, He is the one who told us that we should not live on bread alone, but "on every word that comes from the mouth of God" (Mt. 4:4).

c. Christ's concern for others did not stop Him from allowing them to experience any struggles that were necessary. For example, He purposely allowed Lazarus to die because He wanted to teach Mary and Martha the significance of His resurrection power (Jn. 11:1-44).

Complete Day Five in the Home Study Guide.

VIII. SUMMATION

1. The gift of prophecy entails the ability to size up a situation from the perspective of God's righteousness and truth. This person also has the ability to evaluate people's motives quickly.

2. The gift of serving involves the ability to show love by meeting the pactical needs of others.

3. The gift of teaching is the ability to clarify truth after thorough study and research.

VIII. SUMMATION

4. The gift of exhortation includes the ability to encourage others to grow spiritually, even when they are facing hardship and suffering.

5. The gift of giving is the ability to contribute generously. The giver approaches all of life in terms of giving.

6. The gift of administration involves the ability to coordinate people, resources, and schedules to achieve goals.

7. The gift of mercy is the ability to identify with and comfort those in distress.

103

home study guide

LESSON EIGHT - DAY ONE

SECTIONS I-II

1. Explain the positive and negative aspects of the ministry of the prophet based upon God's call to Jeremiah. Feel free to illustrate your answer with reference to all the prophets of the Old Testament. Jer. 1:1-19

   _____

   _____

   _____

   _____

   _____

2. Write a paragraph to distinguish between the support gift of the prophet, the motivational gift of prophecy, and the supernatural manifestation of prophecy.

   _____

   _____

   _____

   _____

   _____

   _____

3. Review the characteristics of people who possess the motivational gift of prophecy and then identify as many of these as you can in the life of John the Baptist. Lk. 3:3-20

   _____

   _____

   _____

   _____

   _____

4. Can you describe a person you know who is a server? How do they match up with the list of characteristics given in the lesson?

   _____

   _____

   _____

   _____

   _____

   _____

103

home study guide

LESSON EIGHT - DAY TWO

SECTIONS II-III

1. a. Analyze Martha in light of the strengths and weaknesses of the serving gift. Lk. 10:38-42; Jn. 12:2

_____

_____

_____

_____

_____

_____

_____

b. Why would Martha allow herself to be distracted from Jesus to serve? v. 40

_____

_____

c. Why did Martha get upset with Mary?

_____

_____

d. What could Martha have been looking for when she approached Jesus about Mary? v. 40

_____

_____

e. How does Christ's response reveal Martha's interest in only short-term goals? vv. 41-42

_____

_____

_____

_____

2. Review the strengths and weaknesses pertaining to the teaching gift and then analyze Paul's ministry and character as revealed through his epistles to see what characteristics of the teacher he possessed.

_____

_____

_____

_____

_____

_____

208

103

home study guide

LESSON EIGHT · DAY THREE

SECTIONS III-IV

1. Do you know someone who has the motivational gift of teaching? In what ways would the list of weaknesses of the teacher's gift help you to be more sympathetic toward this person and more open to their ministry?

_____

_____

_____

_____

2. Compare and contrast the characteristics of the people with the gift of exhortation and those with the motivational gift of teaching and prophecy.

Exhortation	Teaching	Prophecy
_____	_____	_____
_____	_____	_____
_____	_____	_____
_____	_____	_____

3. Reread the strengths and weaknesses of the exhortation gift and analyze Barnabas in light of the points mentioned. Acts 9:22-27, 11:19-26, 13:43, 14:19-22, 15:35-39 with 12:25 and 13:13.

_____

_____

_____

_____

_____

_____

_____

4. What was the meaning of Barnabas' name and how does this reflect upon his motivational gift? Acts 4:36

_____

_____

5. Describe someone you know who seems to have the gift of exhortation.

_____

_____

_____

_____

_____

103

home study guide

LESSON EIGHT · DAY FOUR

SECTIONS V-VI

1. Describe some of the ways Abraham manifested the motivational gift of giving. Gen. 13:1-11, 14:1-24

   _____
   _____
   _____
   _____
   _____

2. In what way does Genesis 13:2, taken together with 2 Corinthians 9:6, serve to confirm the fact that Abraham's gift was giving?

   _____
   _____
   _____

3. If Abraham thought God required it, how far was he willing to go in his giving? Gen. 22:1-14

   _____

4. Like most people with this gift, Abraham valued something else in his life far more highly than money. What was it? Gen. 15:1

   _____

5. Analyze Nehemiah in terms of the strengths and weaknesses of the administrative gift.

   a. 2:1-16 _____

   _____

   b. ch. 3, 7:5 _____

   _____

   c. 4:1-13 _____

   _____

   d. 7:1-2, 14:30-31 _____

   _____

6. Can you describe someone you know who has the gift of administration?

   _____
   _____
   _____

home study guide

LESSON EIGHT · DAY FIVE

SECTION VII

1. Reread the strengths and weaknesses of the gift of mercy and analyze the Good Samaritan briefly in the light of these factors. Lk. 10:30-37

   _____

   _____

   _____

   _____

   _____

2. Beside each motivational gift mentioned below, quote a scripture which calls upon all believers to show forth the qualities of that gift to some extent even if it is not their primary motivation.

   a. Prophecy

   _____

   _____

   b. Serving

   _____

   _____

   c. Teaching

   _____

   _____

   d. Exhortation

   _____

   _____

   e. Giving

   _____

   _____

   f. Administration

   _____

   _____

   g. Mercy

   _____

   _____

LESSON NINE · KEEPING THE LOCAL CHURCH HEALTHY

OUTLINE

Lesson Nine Update

Lesson Nine Synopsis

I. **INTRODUCTION**

II. **GOD'S PRESCRIPTION FOR A HEALTHY CHURCH**
   A. Step One: Equip the Saints
   B. Step Two: Every Person Ministering
   C. Step Three: Outreach

III. **A HEALTHY CHURCH EQUIPS**
   A. What Does Equipping Involve?
   B. Equipping Involves Discipleship
   C. Equipping Involves Surrender
   D. Equipping Involves Teaching
   E. Equipping Involves Kingdom Socialization
   F. Equipping Involves Service

IV. **A HEALTHY CHURCH INVOLVES EVERY MEMBER IN MINISTRY**
   A. Introduction
   B. Every Member Functioning

V. **A HEALTHY CHURCH REACHES OUT**
   A. Fishers of Men
   B. Two Types of People
   C. The Church's Commission
   D. The Believer's Responsibility

VI. **SUMMATION**

Home Study Guide

LESSON NINE - KEEPING THE LOCAL CHURCH HEALTHY

LESSON NINE UPDATE

Lesson One	God wants His children to be merciful as He is, both in attitude as well as actions.
Lesson Two	Jesus Christ was God's mercy in action identifying fully with man so that He could bring God's recreative life to man for time and eternity.
Lesson Three	Christ trained the apostles, then commissioned and empowered the Church they would build to bring the Good News of redemption and restoration to the world.
Lesson Four	The Church is Christ's body on earth, the living extension of His life and ministry among men even to this day.
Lesson Five	Each member of the Church by means of his spiritual gifts must allow the life and power of Christ to flow through him to the world.
Lesson Six	The four ministries of apostle, prophet, evangelist, and pastor-teacher form the basic life-support system of the body of Christ.
Lesson Seven	Every believer has been given a basic motivational gift that determines the way in which he will approach his ministry in the body of Christ. These gifts include prophecy, serving, teaching, exhortation, organization, giving, and showing mercy.
Lesson Eight	Jesus Christ, our great example, illustrates for us the strengths of each of the seven motivational gifts. He models them for us, however, without their accompanying weaknesses and thus, as we become more like Jesus, we shall overcome the weaknesses of our own motivational gift and exercise it more effectively.

LESSON NINE · KEEPING THE LOCAL CHURCH HEALTHY

LESSON NINE SYNOPSIS

The Church has been called to be Jesus Christ to the world. She is to be the channel of God's mercy. The Church is also the means by which the world is introduced to the restorative life of God, that divine life which alone can replace the brokenness of sin with true health and wholeness.

If the Church is to be this channel of God's mercy and wholeness, her members must themselves, as a result of experiencing the re-creative life of Jesus Christ, be whole. The body of Christ must be healthy if it is to radiate God's mercy and life to a fallen world.

God Himself is the source of the body's health and wholeness. It is only as the local body prepares every believer to be a vital channel of life to the world that it will be truly healthy. It is only as every member becomes actively involved in ministering God's mercy to the world that a local church will become the healthy and vital extension of Jesus Christ which God intends it to be.

LESSON NINE · KEEPING THE LOCAL CHURCH HEALTHY

I. INTRODUCTION

I. INTRODUCTION

God is vitally concerned with the edification (building up) of each local body of believers so that it attains and then maintains prime state of spiritual health. When a local church is not healthy, its effectiveness in outreach and ministry, its effectiveness in being Christ's body on earth is greatly diminished.

II. GOD'S PRESCRIPTION FOR A HEALTHY CHURCH

A. Step One: Equip the Saints

The four supportive leadership gifts equip committed individuals in the local church and bring them into a place of stability, maturity, and preparedness for effective ministry. The word *equip* in Ephesians 4:12 means taking something that is unusable and making it usable.

Ephesians 4:11-12
It was he who gave some to be apostles, some to be prophets, some to be evangelists, and some to be pastors and teachers, ¹²to prepare God's people for works of service, so that the body of Christ may be built up.

B. Step Two: Every Person Ministering

1. The saints once equipped are to serve or minister to one another by means of their spiritual gifts (1 Pet. 4:10). Your predominant motivational gift will usually dictate the manner in which you minister to the other members of the body.

1 Peter 4:10
Each one should use whatever gift he has received to serve others, faithfully administering God's grace in its various forms.

2. Each person must allow the power of the Holy Spirit to flow through him if his gifts, talents, and areas of ministry are to be truly effective (John 7:38-39).

C. Step Three: Outreach

John 7:38-39
"Whoever believes in me, as the Scripture has said, streams of living water will flow from within him." ³⁹By this he meant the Spirit, whom those who believed in him were later to receive. Up to that time the Spirit had not been given, since Jesus had not yet been glorified.

1. The local expression of Christ's body, through its individual members, is to reach out as the full expression of Christ to a fallen world. This can only be done effectively if the body remains in good health.

2. When the local church is in this state of divine health, the life of God can flow to the world through the local body. Without this divine health, the work of God through that local body is severely limited.

LESSON NINE - KEEPING THE LOCAL CHURCH HEALTHY

III. A HEALTHY CHURCH EQUIPS

3. The continued ministry of Christ on earth can be maintained only through a mature and healthy local body of believers.

III. A HEALTHY CHURCH EQUIPS

A. What Does Equipping Involve?

There are basically five aspects to the equipping process:

1. Discipleship
2. Surrender
3. Teaching
4. Socialization
5. Service

B. Equipping Involves Discipleship

1. The local church cannot place enough emphasis upon its primary goal of making disciples (Mt. 28:19-20, refer to *Pathway 101,* Lesson 2). The church, like Christ, must say first to every believer: "Follow the Master."

2. The call must constantly go forth from the pulpit and from the example of leaders and others in the congregation. People must be taught commitment through what they hear and see.

3. This commitment can be nothing short of the total commitment Jesus Christ required in Matthew 16:24-25.

4. There must also be a meaningful way for people to respond. There must be some sort of training program that exposes people to kingdom principles and challenges them to obey the Word as the Holy Spirit makes it clear to them. In other words, people must be shown how to become disciples. The LLI 100 series discipleship program is designed to assist a church in the calling and the developing of mature disciples.

Matthew 28:19-20
"Therefore go and make disciples of all nations, baptizing them in the name of the Father and of the Son and of the Holy Spirit, 20and teaching them to obey everything I have commanded you. And surely I will be with you always, to the very end of the age."

Matthew 16:24-25
Then Jesus said to his disciples, "If anyone would come after me, he must deny himself and take up his cross and follow me. 25For whoever wants to save his life will lose it, but whoever loses his life for me will find it."

LESSON NINE · KEEPING THE LOCAL CHURCH HEALTHY

III. A HEALTHY CHURCH EQUIPS

Hebrew 12:6-11

"Because the Lord disciplines those he loves and he punishes everyone he accepts as a son."

[7]Endure hardship as discipline; God is treating you as sons. For what son is not disciplined by his father? [8]If you are not disciplined (and everyone undergoes discipline), then you are illegitimate children and not true sons. [9]Moreover, we have all had human fathers who disciplined us and we respected them for it. How much more should we submit to the Father of our spirits and live! [10]Our fathers disciplined us for a little while as they thought best; but God disciplines us for our good, that we may share in his holiness [11]No discipline seems pleasant at the time, but painful. Later on, however, it produces a harvest of righteousness and peace for those who have been trained by it.

Romans 8:15-17

For you did not receive a spirit that makes you a slave again to fear, but you received the Spirit of sonship. And by him we cry, "*Abba*, Father." [16]The Spirit himself testifies with our spirit that we are God's children. [17]Now if we are children, then we are heirs—heirs of God and co-heirs with Christ, if indeed we share in his sufferings in order that we may also share in his glory.

Romans 12:1

Therefore, I urge you, brothers, in view of God's mercy, to offer your bodies as living sacrifices, holy and pleasing to God—which is your spiritual worship.

2 Corinthians 4:10

We always carry around in our body the death of Jesus, so that the life of Jesus may also be revealed in our body.

C. Equipping Involves Surrender

1. A local church must emphasize the need for yielding to the maturing discipline of God in discipleship. There is always the temptation to eliminate the workings of the cross principle in every believer's life (see *Pathway 101*, Lessons 7, 8, and 9). Without the testings of God, however, there can be no real growth or preparation for ministry (Heb. 12:6-11).

2. The ultimate end of surrender, however, is life, abundant and eternal. The call to discipleship, should always emphasize the ultimate blessings of the kingdom that belong to every disciple. Those who live the committed life always experience these blessings as Jesus said: "Whoever loses his life for me will find it" (Mt. 16:25).

   a. Many, because of their endurance and persistence will, through faith, receive many of the blessings of the kingdom in this life (Heb. 11:29-35a).

   b. Others, however, because of their circumstances have been chosen to await the fuller blessings of the kingdom in the life to come (Heb. 11:35b-40). All will eventually receive Christ's abundance as joint heirs with Him (Ro. 8:15-17).

3. Equipping cannot really begin until Romans 12:1 is part of the believer's experience. Each individual is asked by God to give his or her life over to the Father's molding process. We are to offer our lives as a living sacrifice, dying to self and letting God deal a death blow to the carnal nature so that the resurrected life of His Spirit can flow forth from our innermost being (2 Cor. 4:10).

D. Equipping Involves Teaching

1. Jesus (the Word made flesh) proclaimed the Word of God to men. His Word healed, restored, and renewed human beings.

2. So it is today. The Word must be preached, taught, and received. It is the Word of God that imparts life to the individual members of the body and the world.

LESSON NINE · KEEPING THE LOCAL CHURCH HEALTHY

III. A HEALTHY CHURCH EQUIPS

3. The Word must go forth in the power of the Spirit. Men and women, whose inner eyes have been illumined to understand, must teach in the power of the Holy Spirit.

4. The church is a Christian educational center and should provide teaching in several ways:

   a. The pastor must be given the time he needs to fulfill God's role for his life. Before anything else, the pastor is to be a teacher. If a congregation will not allow a pastor to spend enough of his time in preparation for ministry, perhaps because of the heavy administrative burden he may be forced to carry alone, then that congregation is not serious about equipping or discipleship. Likewise, if the pastor does not discipline himself to spend several hours each day in study, then this vital equipping and discipling aspect of his ministry will suffer.

   b. There must be a strong, goal-oriented program of adult education that fulfills the following objectives:

      (1) Establish people in the foundational concepts of discipleship and Christian living.

      (2) Continue to effectively equip people with a more thorough understanding of the Bible as their Christian lives develop. People should be part of a program that gives them a book-by-book, chapter-by-chapter, verse-by-verse understanding of the Word of God.

5. The very word *discipleship* comes from the root word discipline. The church cannot underestimate the importance of each member disciplining himself in regard to biblical training and study. The church in our modern age has for the most part allowed the lackadaisical attitude of society toward learning dictate its training programs. This more than anything else may account for the lack of sincere dedication on behalf of many church members.

Pathway of Discipleship

LESSON NINE · KEEPING THE LOCAL CHURCH HEALTHY

III. A HEALTHY CHURCH EQUIPS

E. Equipping Involves Kingdom Socialization

1. The Church is God's kingdom on earth. It is totally distinct in character from the kingdom of this world. It is like a culture within a culture. The ultimate light of Christ is demonstrated when the world sees the culture of God's kingdom shining through the lives of the members of His Church on earth.

2. It is imperative, therefore, that Christians be socialized to take on the character of the divine culture: the kingdom of God.

3. A child is socialized in the home (see *Pathway 101*, Lesson 6). He is a product of all the experience he has gone through while being a member of a particular family. A person's values, attitudes, and philosophy of life are largely a result of what he has learned in the home. So it is in the kingdom of God. A Christian learns the likeness of Christ from a knowledge of the Word and from the spiritual culture he grows up in.

4. The proper climate:

   a. Whereas the family serves as the proper climate for a child to reach maturity as a member of his own national culture, so the small weekly cell group plays the most significant role in the socialization of the Christian.

   b. Dr. Lawrence Richards points out that there are five requisites for effective socialization education in the kingdom:

      (1) People (i.e., the group members) whose lives serve as models or examples of the teachings of Scripture.

      (2) Discussion about the teachings of Scripture.

      (3) Identification by the learner with others who also have struggles and problems.

      (4) Deeply caring interpersonal relationships.

III. A HEALTHY CHURCH EQUIPS

(5) Sharing in each others lives so that the Christian life-style is seen manifested in various ways through various people.[1]

c. Dr. Richards goes on to say the following about small groups:

> The significance of the small grouping in the Church is simply this: it provides the optimum setting for meeting all or most of the five requisites for effective "socialization" education![2]

d. The church has a great responsibility to provide this small group context for effective socialization education as Dr. Richards points out:

> How does a Christian learn *his* likeness? How does he grow and change, learning the divine perceptions, attitudes, emotions, values and behaviors? If likeness is our concern—if discipling is our goal—then we need to focus our educational efforts not on isolated verbalizations of Truth, but on shaping a community in which Truth is lived as reality. We need to focus our educational efforts on understanding and using the Church, the Body of Christ, as a culture within which persons who receive the gift of God's life are to be involved, and through this involvement be *socialized* into all that it means to become like Him.[3]

F. Equipping Involves Service

1. The church must stress that faith without works is dead. People must be challenged to and recruited for service. A strong emphasis on teaching in the local church is fruitless if it does not result in ministry involvement. The equipping process must produce results. Therefore, every member is to begin to function once he has been equipped to do a work of service.

2. One of the key problems is that most churches are very limited in their organizational structure. They are not flexible enough to be constantly adding new areas of ministry as the body expands. (Refer to Lesson 5, Section III, C.)

---

[1] Adapted from Lawrence O. Richards, *A Theology of Christian Education* (Zondervan Publishing House, 1975), p. 251.
[2] Richards, p. 265.
[3] Richards, pp. 77-78.

IV. A HEALTHY CHURCH INVOLVES EVERY MEMBER

3. An effective personnel recruitment and placement service is essential for a healthy local church. Forms have been included following this week's home study guide to show you how churches can begin to recruit and place people in leadership positions. Complete these forms and give them to your group leader. If your church does not have a deacon in charge of ministry placement (one who can take your form and effectively place you in service), you should encourage your pastor to inaugurate such a ministry.

The recruitment and placement service is one of the most important areas of ministry in a local body. In fact, LLI recommends that a full-time member be added to the staff of larger churches to direct such a recruitment and placement office right in the church.

IV. A HEALTHY CHURCH INVOLVES EVERY MEMBER IN MINISTRY

A. Introduction

1. This section includes a diagram taken from *Pathway 102*, Lesson 5. It is reproduced here in order to refresh your memory concerning how a local church should be structured for specialized ministry.

2. Each person in the church should, for the most part, be committed to:

   a. A weekly worship service.
   b. A weekly cell group.
   c. One area of specialized ministry.

3. Depending on the circumstances, commitment to regular church involvement beyond the above-mentioned areas is questionable because the individual's spiritual life and family life might suffer.

4. In light of what has been discussed in this lesson, a ministry area of personnel recruitment and placement has been added to the diagram that follows.

LESSON NINE · KEEPING THE LOCAL CHURCH HEALTHY

IV. A HEALTHY CHURCH INVOLVES EVERY MEMBER

B. Every Member Functioning

1. Diagram

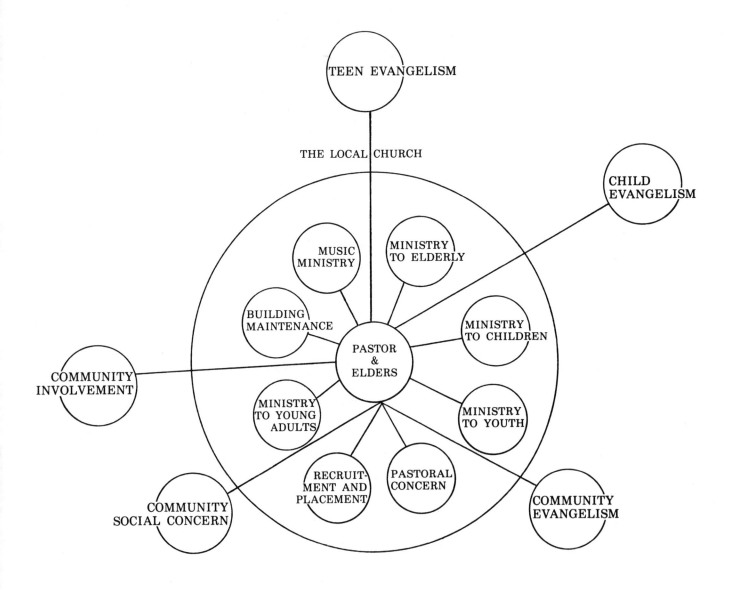

2. Diagram Explanation

a. The local church (largest circle) can be viewed as having an ever-increasing number of ministry teams.

b. Each team is headed by a deacon or deaconess. Certain ministry areas may need more than one deacon, depending on their size and diversity of activity.

c. Certain ministry teams perform services within the local body. These are represented within the large circle of the diagram, e.g., building maintenance, music, and so forth.

d. Other ministry teams perform outreach services to the community. These are represented outside the large circle of the diagram, e.g., teen evangelism, community involvement, social concern, and so forth.

e. Each church will be able to expand into new ministry areas as qualified leadership becomes available. (Refer to *Pathway 101*, Lesson 3.)

f. Every member should become part of a specific ministry team, utilizing whatever spiritual gifts God has given him. In so doing he must be willing to follow the leadership of the deacon in charge.

g. Because of the higher priority of family life over church involvement, no individual should be involved in more than one ministry team. An exception would be a single person who is devoting all of his free time to the Lord's work.

V. A HEALTHY CHURCH REACHES OUT

A. Fishers of Men

In this section some notes from *Fishers of Men*, Lesson 1 have been included to show the ultimate importance of a local body reaching out in ministry to the world.

LESSON NINE · KEEPING THE LOCAL CHURCH HEALTHY

V. A HEALTHY CHURCH REACHES OUT

Acts 21:8
Leaving the next day, we reached Caesarea and stayed at the house of Philip the evangelist, one of the Seven.

Luke 12:8
"I tell you, whoever acknowledges me before men, the Son of Man will also acknowledge him before the angels of God."

John 20:21
Again Jesus said, "Peace be with you! As the Father has sent me, I am sending you."

Luke 4:18-19
"The Spirit of the Lord is on me, because he has anointed me to preach good news to the poor.
He has sent me to proclaim freedom for the prisoners
and recovery of sight for the blind,
to release the oppressed,
19 to proclaim the year of the Lord's favor."

Acts 3:19-21
Repent, then, and turn to God, so that your sins may be wiped out, that times of refreshing may come from the Lord, 20 and that he may send the Christ, who has been appointed for you—even Jesus. 21 He must remain in heaven until the time comes for God to restore everything, as he promised long ago through his holy prophets.

Revelation 21:1-4
"Then I saw a new heaven and a new earth, for the first heaven and the first earth had passed away, and there was no longer any sea. 2 I saw the Holy City, the new Jerusalem, coming down out of heaven from God, prepared as a bride beautifully dressed for her husband. 3 And I heard a loud voice from the throne saying, "Now the dwelling of God is with men, and he will live with them. They will be his people, and God himself will be with them and be their God. 4 He will wipe every tear from their eyes. There will be no more death or mourning or crying or pain, for the old order of things has passed away."

B. Two Types of People

1. There are those individuals who have been called to a specific ministry of evangelistic outreach. Their task is to constantly proclaim the gospel, persuading men to accept Jesus Christ. Peter had this gift and so did Philip, one of the first deacons (Acts 2:14-41, 21:8).

2. There are many others in the body of Christ who support the front-line evangelistic operation. In a regular army there is an extensive support system backing up those in combat. It is important to note, however, that all military personnel have gone through basic training and could be called to the front at any moment. So it is with the body of Christ. No one can excuse himself from learning the skills of leading people to Jesus Christ. Many may not have a specific front-line gift of evangelism, but God may call them to the front at any time to articulate the gospel to a hurting friend or neighbor. Scripture emphasizes that being a witness for Christ is part of what it means to be a Christian (Lk. 12:8).

C. The Church's Commission

The Church is called to continue the mission of Jesus Christ by proclaiming the gospel until all men hear. Jesus said to the disciples, in the same way that the Father had sent Him into the world, so He was sending them (Jn. 20:21). Thus, the proclamation of Luke 4:18-19 is as vital today as it was at the inauguration of the earthly ministry of Jesus Christ (see pp. 49-50). The Church is called as a body to proclaim and demonstrate the hope of the Christian gospel to all men who are poor, enslaved, and oppressed. Every local church is to actually open the doors of God's truth and power upon the world. It is to preach, with signs accompanying, that the Lord's kingdom of total restoration in the world to come can be tasted and experienced by all men even now. It is to make men aware that what we enjoy through Christ now is but a foretaste of God's complete work of restoration in the age to come (Acts 3:19-21; Rev. 21:1-4).

LESSON NINE · KEEPING THE LOCAL CHURCH HEALTHY

VI. SUMMATION

D. The Believer's Responsibility

1. As a believer in Christ, you are one of the members of His body, the Church. It is of utmost importance for you to understand your responsibility or function as it relates to Christ's overall commission to His Church. The question then is, Where do I fit in?

2. As we have studied, every believer has been given a particular gift and place of ministry in the local church. Your gift or gifts, however, must always relate to the overall commission of Christ to His Church. Just as an army is out to win the battle, the supreme task of the Church is to win the world. Every true disciple must see himself as part of the total outreach of his local church to the world. To lose the vision for a lost world simply because one's gift is not specifically of an evangelistic or front-line nature is to let the Church die. The growing churches of the world are the churches that live and breathe evangelism. A church that is burning with the desire on the part of its membership to reach the world and make disciples of all men is flowing in line with Christ's desire and commission.

VI. SUMMATION

1. God is the source of all life, health, and wholeness in the lives of individual believers as well as the Church. Therefore, only when a church is following God's prescription will there be a healthy local body.

2. Healthy churches equip the saints for ministry, involve every member in ministry, and reach out to meet the physical, social, and spiritual needs of their community.

3. In order to equip people, a healthy church must emphasize the importance of personal discipleship. This requires teaching, encouraging people to commit themselves fully to Christ's Lordship, providing a small group context for socialization in kingdom principles, and involving growing disciples in Christian service.

LESSON NINE · KEEPING THE LOCAL CHURCH HEALTHY

VI. SUMMATION

4. In order to be truly healthy, a local church must strive to challenge, train, and involve every one of its members in ministry based upon individual spiritual gifts.

5. Healthy churches constantly emphasize the believer's responsibility in personal evangelism. They point out that every gift must work together toward the goal of making disciples among the nations through the proclamation and demonstration of the gospel.

103

home study guide

LESSON NINE

You have already been exposed to much of the material in this lesson. This week's home study questions, therefore, will entail thoughtful reflection in preparation for your last discussion.

Also included is a leadership questionnaire that you should prayerfully fill out. This form will be held in strict confidence by the leadership of the church and is designed to assist you in finding and fulfilling your role in the body of Christ. After you fill out the questionnaire, please give it to the cell group leader in a sealed envelope to be passed on to the pastoral leadership of your church.

Because this week's home study guide is of such a different nature, we have not designated any specific days to the study.

103

home study guide

LESSON NINE

1. What are the three things essential for a healthy church?

    (1) _____

    (2) _____

    (3) _____

2. List and briefly describe the five basic aspects of the equipping process.

    (1) _____

    _____

    _____

    _____

    (2) _____

    _____

    _____

    _____

    (3) _____

    _____

    _____

    _____

    (4) _____

    _____

    _____

    _____

    (5) _____

    _____

    _____

    _____

3. Analyze your church in terms of these five aspects of equipping. Suggest ways the church's performance could be improved in each area. This is not a time to be critical of your local church. Make it rather a time of brainstorming for ideas to improve your church's effectiveness.

    (1) _____

    _____

    _____

    _____

home study guide

LESSON NINE

(2) _____

_____

_____

_____

_____

_____

(3) _____

_____

_____

_____

_____

_____

(4) _____

_____

_____

_____

_____

_____

_____

(5) _____

_____

_____

_____

_____

_____

4. Reread Section IV on every member functioning and briefly describe how your church could improve its organizational structure in order to facilitate ministry involvement on the part of every member. _____

_____

_____

_____

_____

_____

103

home study guide

LESSON NINE

5. What do you think of the concept of front-line and supportive gifts of evangelism? Which category do you belong in?

_____

_____

_____

_____

_____

_____

6. In your opinion, how can your local church become more effective in its outreach to the community?

_____

_____

_____

_____

_____

_____

_____

_____

_____

7. Now that you have completed _Pathway 103_, briefly summarize your understanding of what it means to be merciful, especially with reference to the role of the Church of Jesus Christ in this world.

_____

_____

_____

_____

_____

_____

_____

_____

_____

PRAYER LIST

"Ask and it will be given to you; seek and you will find; knock and the door will be opened to you. For everyone who asks receives; he who seeks finds; and to him who knocks, the door will be opened."   (Matthew 7:7-8)

Pray over each request briefly each day until God answers.

NAME	REQUEST	DATE ASKED	DATE ANSWERED

Local Church Ministry Involvement Questionnaire

This questionnaire will enable the church leadership and placement service to understand you and your place of ministry better. Hopefully, it will also help you specifically outline for yourself the areas of ministry in which you want to be involved.

Personal Information

Name_____ Phone_____

Street_____ Date of Birth_____

City_____ Zip_____

Occupation_____ Sex_____

Married_____ Single_____ Widow(er)_____ Divorced_____

Place a recent picture of
yourself (and your spouse)
here.

Spiritual Life and Experience

Date Converted_____ Date of water baptism_____ How often do you pray?_____

Do you have a regular systematic Bible reading plan? _____ Are you in agreement with the basic doctrines of the church? _____ If not, please specify. _____

_____

_____

What LLI Evangelism Nurture Courses have you completed?   Y.A.W. _____   F.T.F. _____

_____

What LLI Discipleship courses have you completed?   NLS____101____102____103____104____FOM____

What other training have you received through church seminars, conventions, etc.?_____

_____

_____

List other LLI Ministry Training Courses: _____

_____

_____

List your educational experience – special Bible or other courses, diplomas, degrees, areas of expertise, seminars, etc. _____

_____

_____

_____

Do you see any of your expertise in the secular world applicable to the local church ministry? If so, explain.

_____

_____

_____

_____

_____

Family Information

Name of Spouse_____ Occupation _____ Date of Birth_____

Is he/she a Christian?_____ Has he/she been divorced?_____ Have you discussed with him/her the responsibilities and privileges of ministry at your local church?_____ What is his/her attitude?_____

_____

_____

Names and ages of children _____

_____

Relationships

Are you an active member of your local church?_____ How long have you been a member?_____

Do you attend every week?_____

Do you support the church regularly and systematically with your tithes and offerings?_____ Are you a member of a small group? _____ If so, who is your group leader?_____

What is your understanding of submission to local church authority? _____

_____

_____

_____

_____

_____

_____

Is there any person with whom you have problems relating? (Explain) _____

_____

_____

_____

_____

_____

Would you have any problem submitting to the leadership of the church?_____
If so, please explain. _____

_____

_____

_____

_____

Do you understand that leadership is a privilege and demands sacrifice, and a willingness to serve the Lord by serving the Lord's people? _____

Ministry Gifts and Talents

List what talents you feel you could contribute to the ministry of the local church. _____

_____

_____

_____

What area of ministry do you feel you would like to serve in most?_____

_____

_____

List ministries you have been involved in over the years. _____

_____

_____

_____

_____

_____

Please list how much you feel you can be involved in a specialized ministry (i.e., one night, two nights, a Saturday, etc.) _____

_____

What is your present involvement in specialized ministry? Please list weekly activities. _____

_____

_____

_____

_____

If you are recognized as a leader for ministry, would you be willing to assist or serve on probation for a period?

_____

Equip Yourself for Service in the Body of Christ

LAY LEADERSHIP INTERNATIONAL

As a Christian you have a special place, a ministry to fulfill. LLI courses will help you discover your own unique gifts and God-given calling.

 ### Pre-level Studies

First Things First is an exciting, 28-lesson study on Christian growth. Its purpose is to help every follower of Christ realize what God wants them to be in many practical areas of life. Each lesson enables you to dig into the Bible and learn the priorities God wants His children to follow.

LLI'S LOCAL CHURCH INSTITUTE CURRICULUM
Intensive 9-week courses in Discipleship

 ### Level-One Studies

New Life Studies is a study of the foundational truths of the Christian life. It deals with such key topics as salvation, assurance, the Bible, prayer, handling your problems, and sharing your faith. Experience has shown that believers both young and old in the faith profit greatly from this course.

 ### Level-Two Studies

Pathway of Discipleship 101 and *102* are the first two in a series of four courses that make an intensive study of the Beatitudes. In these eight short statements, Jesus sets forth for every disciple the essential principles of His Kingdom. *Pathway 101* begins by examining the importance of the local church as the place where disciples are truly formed. It also deals with learning to depend upon God (spiritual poverty) and the methods God uses to make us like Christ (spiritual mourning). *Pathway 102* continues with an extensive study of how the Christian relates to divine as well as human authority (meekness) and the key motivation underlying all discipleship: spiritual hunger.

 ### Level-Three Studies

Pathway 103 continues the series with an in-depth examination of the subject of mercy. It deals with the Church as the body of Christ on earth becoming the total expression of Christ's love and ministry to a broken world. Included in this course are helpful insights on how the believer can discover, develop, and deploy his spiritual gifts through the body of Christ to the glory of God. *Pathway 104* begins by examining purity, the essential quality of discipleship. It continues with the theme, "blessed are the peacemakers" and shows how the unity of the Church is essential to her witness to the world. The Pathway series concludes with a look at persecution, the inevitable reaction to discipleship as well as the ways in which every Christian can become the salt of the earth and the light of the world.

 ### Level-Four Studies

Fishers of Men is a 9-week course providing basic training in personal evangelism. It clearly explains what the gospel is and how to present it. Here is a wholistic approach to evangelism that emphasizes loving and consistent involvement in ministering to the needs of people as an integral part of winning them to Christ. This course includes practical training in personal evangelism through the use of role playing in the cell group setting. It also gives instruction in the use of LLI's key tools for evangelism and new convert nurture: *You Are Welcome* and *First Things First.*